E. GLENN WAGNER PH.D

THE AWESOME POWER OF SHARED BELIEFS

WORD PUBLISHING
Dallas · London · Vancouver · Melbourne

THE AWESOME POWER OF SHARED BELIEFS

Unless otherwise indicated, Scripture quotations in this book are from the Holy Bible, New International Version (NIV). Copyright © 1973, 1978, 1984 International Bible Society. Used by permission of Zondervan Bible Publishers. Other Scripture references are from the following sources:

The King James Version of the Bible (KJV).

The Message (TM), copyright © 1993. Used by permission of NavPress Publishing Group.

The New American Standard (NASB) © 1960, 1962, 1963, 1968, 1971, 1972, 1973, 1975, 1977 by The Lockman Foundation. Used by permission.

The New King James Version (NKJV). Copyright © 1979, 1980, 1982, 1990, Thomas Nelson, Inc., Publisher.

The Revised Standard Version of the Bible (RSV). Copyright © 1946, 1952, 1971, 1973 by the Division of Christian Education of the National Council of the Churches of Christ in the U.S.A. Used by permission.

Library of Congress Cataloging-in-Publication Data
Wagner, E. Glenn, 1953–
The awesome power of shared beliefs / Glenn Wagner.
p. cm.
ISBN 0-8499-1213-X
1. Theology, Doctrinal Popular works. 2. Men—Religious life. 3. Church—Unity.
I. Title.
BT77.W248   1995
230' .081–dc20   95-6919
                                                                         CIP

Printed in the United States of America
5 6 7 8 0 1 2 3 9 BVG 9 8 7 6 5 4 3 2

CONTENTS

Foreword

Randy T. Phillips
President, Promise Keepers

We in the Body of Christ are experiencing something today that is quite unique. Never before in our nation's history have so many from such varied backgrounds been drawn together in evangelistic outreach, Christ-centered discipleship teaching, and corporate worship. While this broad-based realignment is unprecedented in the record of our culture, it is not unprecedented in biblical history. It was the Lord Himself, after all, who raised up the twelve distinct tribes of Israel for the purpose of showing unity in diversity. It was a fascinating initiative from which one might conclude that God took a calculated risk. In His knowledge of the human heart, God understood absolutely how twelve separate tribes would either reflect the penetrating strength diversity brings to congregational expressions of worship and service—or it would breed division. Scripture reveals that God's heart was for His people to rise above their prejudices and human propensities for division and embrace their true destiny—that of a mighty nation uniquely appointed to glorify God. In three familiar Jewish celebrations—Passover, Pentecost, and the Feast of Tabernacles—the rallying together of all Jews held far greater significance than family, village, or tribe. It sealed Israel's identity as a nation pledged in common commitment to the Almighty God of Israel.

New challenges to the unity of believers came with the formation of the New Testament Church. On numerous occasions the Apostle Paul sought to bring down dividing walls of hostility among the brethren. In fact, much of the Book of Ephesians targets this theme. Ephesians 2: 13–14 reads: "But now in Christ Jesus you who once were far off have been made near by the blood of Christ. For He Himself is our peace, who has made both one, and has broken down the middle wall of division between us." The Gospel continually reinforces God's commitment to unite His Body.

Today the church still wrestles with the tension of tribal distinctives. Various denominations have their own uncompromising convictions that mirror their God-given uniqueness. Yet Scripture reminds us of God's heart: uniqueness must ultimately flow into unity. In *The Awesome Power of Shared Beliefs*, our authors examine carefully the five foundational convictions all who would call themselves Christians *must* agree upon: 1. The inerrancy of the Word of God; 2. The nature and attributes of God; 3. The Person and deity of Jesus Christ; 4. The role of the Holy Spirit in our salvation, and 5. Redemption and salvation through Jesus Christ. Nothing illustrates this principle more clearly than what has occurred within Promise Keepers. Men from clearly distinct "tribal" backgrounds are also sharing basic, unshakable convictions. It is conviction tempered by compassion. By discovering what we can all agree upon, men are brought out of isolation. They are finding affirmation and accountability in small groups—and many are showing more interest in helping to support the mission of the local church. Likewise, our churches are less isolated and are reaching out to an unbelieving community with greater impact.

Psalm 133 says, "Behold how good and pleasant it is when brothers dwell together in unity." It goes on to say that . . ."there the Lord bestows his blessing." Blessings flow, then, when brothers really dwell together, not just when they attend Promise Keepers conferences together. The purpose of unity is not for us to feel good about ourselves and our tightknit relationships. Jesus emphasized that His Bride must show unity so that we "may be made perfect in one," and so that "the world may know that You have sent Me, and have loved them as You have loved Me." (John 17: 23) When brothers genuinely dwell together in unity, they witness the love of God to those who don't know His love.

God's presence manifested in the midst of a unified church is also the prerequisite for revival. Following Pentecost the disciples went from house to house breaking bread . . . and the Lord added to the church daily those who were being saved. The church in solidarity brings salvation to the lost. God's sovereign hand calling the unsaved to repentance flows forth in the midst of a unified Body. Where the net is strong, He knows it is safe to send fish to the fishermen. Where the net is torn and fragmented, He knows the fish will only fall through the holes. It has been ordained by God that a unified Body alone is equipped to inherit the lost, and provide support necessary to bring babes in Christ to maturity.

Again and again Scripture teaches us the power of obedience to God's Word. The Body of Christ obeys God's commands by demonstrating a power in human relationships that far exceeds human initiative. The church is to exhibit such unity of purpose and compassion of spirit that the lost are gripped with an undeniable conviction that God alone is responsible. It is a depth of commitment that will see Christians pouring out their lives in service to one another—embodying Jesus' prayer for His beautiful Bride. His church is to be a living, free-flowing expression of sacrificial love, illuminating for a dying world the unmistakable power and authority of Christ's united body. It begins in the heart of one man, then two at a time. I trust *The Awesome Power of Shared Beliefs* will encourage you to put into practice the call to unite with your brothers in Christ.

Acknowledgments

The writing of any book is never a solo endeavor, but even more so in the case of *The Awesome Power of Shared Beliefs.* I want to thank Robert Wolgemuth for believing in this project and for re-connecting me with an old college friend, Bill Butterworth, without whom this book would not have been possible. Bill's incredible gift for writing and editing, his sense of humor that lifted me at just the right time, and his love for the body of Christ have made this book possible.

I also wish to acknowledge the five men who contributed doctrinal chapters with great understanding and clarity.

Dr. Bruce Shelley, distinguished professor of theology at Denver Seminary; Dr. Max Anders, well known for his life-centered biblical teaching and practical insight as both a writer and a speaker; Jeff Van Vonderen, director of Damascus, Inc., and also an author, speaker, and pastor; Dr. Jack Hayford, well-known author and pastor of Church on the Way in Van Nuys, California; and Dr. Rod Cooper, author, speaker, friend, and director of educational ministries for Promise Keepers.

It is a privilege to minister shoulder to shoulder with the men and women of Promise Keepers, but especially those who read and critiqued this manuscript. They are men who seek to live out in their daily lives the truth of this book. To Randy Phillips, Pete Richardson, Rick Kingham, and Dale Schlafer, I say thank you. And I would not have had the time to devote to this project without the help of my executive assistant, Sherry Kuehl.

Also, I would be remiss if I didn't acknowledge three very special people in my life. They are the ones who live with a project-oriented husband and father and do so with great encouragement and affirmation. To my wife, Susan, our daughter, Haven, and our son, Justin, I say thanks for your love. I thank God for each of you.

Introduction

It was truly an awesome experience.

On a beautiful summer's night in Boulder, Colorado, the Colorado University football stadium was overflowing with humanity, all male. Since the night before, these guys had sat and listened to speaker after speaker address topics that were of critical importance to their lives. They had spent time in prayer and worship together. Men of all races, men of every socioeconomic status, men of many denominations, had gathered to share together under the banner of our Lord Jesus Christ.

It was a Promise Keepers conference of memorable proportion. The founder, Bill McCartney, was speaking to the crowd. I've never seen any communicator who had greater effectiveness with men than Coach Mac had that night. He reached a point where he wanted to hammer home one of his points. "The role of pastor is the highest calling in the land," he stated. "I know there are many pastors here tonight, and I think we need to let these guys know how much we appreciate them!" he said. "I want all the pastors to get out of their seats right now and come down here by the front of the platform."

As they started streaming out of their locations all over the stadium, the crowd exploded into spontaneous cheering and applause. The roar was deafening and was heard for miles.

Soon the crowd started chanting, "We love you! We love you!" as the pastors continued to make their way from the stands to the playing field and eventually to the edge of the speakers platform.

Introduction

Dale Schlafer, a fellow staff member, told me later, "Glenn, I was so moved by this expression I could hardly contain myself. After the conference I received the video footage and timed the duration of the ovation. It was absolutely amazing to me. This stadium full of guys applauded their pastors for *twenty-four minutes!*"

This was no mere emotional pep rally brought on by a locker-room half-time get-one-for-the-Gipper kind of speech. Something much more powerful and dramatic had taken place. Men in the stands were affirming the pastors as they made their way to the platform. And the pastors, standing there on the field before the adoring crowd, were so moved by this spontaneous show of appreciation and affirmation that many of them wept openly.

But behind all of this, something even greater was taking place, something the Bible refers to when it speaks of the family of God, or the community of faith. This affirmation and praise sprang forth from lives knit together by a belief—the belief that we really do need each other. The body was lifting up the Body. I can just about guarantee you that any of the thousands of men who attended that event will not soon forget the impact it had on all of us.

A casual glance would confirm that the crowd was made up of a far-reaching tapestry of diversity. Yet in the midst of this diversity, there was true unity. It was more than awesome . . .

It was the awesome power of a shared belief. The Bible talks about unity in the midst of diversity. The apostle Paul used the analogy of a human body to explain this concept. In his first letter to the Christians at Corinth, Paul described it this way:

> The body is a unit, though it is made up of many parts; and though all its parts are many, they form one body. So it is with Christ. (1 Cor. 12:12)

Paul went on to explain we are all different parts of the same body. Feet, elbows, mouths, livers, bellybuttons . . . all diverse but all vital to the makeup of a single human body. As diverse parts, we have different tasks to accomplish, but we are all brought together to relate as one body. Paul clarified this issue in writing to the Romans:

Introduction

> Just as each of us has one body with many members, and these members do not all have the same function, so in Christ we who are many form one body, and each member belongs to all the others. (Rom. 12:4–5)

Don't think for a minute that because the emphasis of this book is on unity we have any intention of shortchanging the importance of diversity. It is of utmost importance to strive for unity, but it is diversity that enhances the unity. Another good human illustration of this concept is marriage.

Susan and I are about as diverse as two people can be. Sometimes I feel like the only thing we hold in common is our Christianity. And even that is not without its differences. She became a Christian in senior high whereas I was not a believer until several years after high school. She comes from a large family, being one of seven kids. I come from a home with two other siblings. She loves tennis. I hate tennis but love God's game—golf. Susan takes great pains to tell stories with every fact, feeling, and great emotion while I tend to be a "just-the-facts" kind of storyteller. She likes Broadway musicals; I enjoy an occasional evening at the opera. She gravitates to middle-of-the-road Christian pop; I really enjoy a solid Christian rock band or jazz. I believe in arriving at every function or appointment with plenty of time to spare, and this makes absolutely no sense to my Susan.

We're different.

But it really is those differences that highlight the fact that we are one. Let's face it: If we were identical, it would be an awfully boring marriage. As someone said, that would mean one of us was unnecessary. So when we speak of the need for unity, it is with an understanding and acceptance of our diversity.

Another way to look at the issue of unity and diversity is to look at the Godhead. There is incredible diversity in the Three in One. Yet even though the Father, the Son, and the Holy Spirit are three distinct Persons with great diversity in their tasks, there is still oneness within the Trinity.

It's the same for Christ's body, the church. There are many people in His body, including you and me. We are all diverse, with different gifts, different talents, different perspectives on issues, different cultures, subcultures, etc. But if we reach the point that we allow our differences to divide us, our power and effectiveness are diminished, and we spend our resources fighting each other. As a result, we will never impact our world in the way God intended.

Greater oneness will make us stronger as we face the issues we must all confront. Unity will make us more effective in meeting the social needs of our world, creating stronger family units, and achieving many of our own personal needs.

The beauty of God's plan is that we were meant to get along with one another in unity while accepting and celebrating our diversity. As you read on, you can see that doctrine is important, both to believe and to practice. The word *doctrine* isn't something to be thought of as frightening or intimidating. When I use that word I mean simply teaching . . . the teaching of the Scriptures.

This book is a compilation of encouraging, insightful writings by men of various backgrounds and church traditions who have, in many cases, spent a lifetime studying the Scriptures to discern God's teachings, his doctrine, for our lives. While the ideas shared here can no doubt be enlightening and inspiring to all readers, they are specifically directed toward men—Christian men, both leaders and followers. My experience—and that of my fellow writers of this book—has been that when men from every part of Christ's body unite around these basic doctrines, exciting things can and will happen.

Part One

The Need for Unity

ChapterOne

Friendly Fire

IT HAPPENED during the war in the Persian Gulf.

It was the night of January 29, 1991, in Saudi Arabia. Lance Corporal Ron Tull was part of the eight-man crew that manned a light armored vehicle (LAV) in Delta Company. Twelve other LAVs were a part of this light armored infantry group that had established a camp thirty-seven miles west of Khafji, a coastal town.

About 10 P.M. the silence of the desert was rudely interrupted by an excited voice over the radio. "L-A-I! L-A-I! This is Recon! Thirty Iraqi tanks are coming over the berm!"

Corporal Tull, better known to his friends as Tully, knew this was it. He and his crew climbed into the LAV, and Tully settled in behind the wheel. His assignment was to keep the vehicle in formation, avoid collision with other LAVs, and watch out for tanks. What made this job especially challenging was that it was to be accomplished while the LAV was speeding across the desert at a clip of fifty miles per hour.

Suddenly a missile from another LAV exploded into an Iraqi tank thirty yards to the left. Just moments later a second tank was hit seventy yards ahead. Fighting this close was unnerving, but Tully's crew swallowed hard and continued to move on with their mission.

No one in Tully's LAV saw the U.S. Air Force A-10 fighter swooping out of the sky behind them in an attack dive. The pilot aimed a heat-seeking missile at an Iraqi tank. But heat radiating from the LAV's guns and rear exhaust confused the missile's guidance system. It altered course abruptly and fired into the left rear of Tully's LAV.

The explosion blew the gun turret off and threw the LAV into the air like a tin can hit by a shotgun blast. Tully felt bomb fragments penetrate his back, the force of the explosion slamming him into the steering wheel and then throwing him out of the vehicle onto the desert sand.

His face black with burns, his back fractured in three places, Tully miraculously stumbled fifteen yards from the vehicle before collapsing facedown in the sand. When he came to in the hospital, he was informed that he was the only one of his crew to survive. The other seven marines in the rear of the LAV were killed instantly . . . by their own comrades.

It's called "friendly fire."[1]

A story like that leaves me with a horribly uncomfortable feeling. Everybody knows it's not supposed to work that way. Unfortunately, that's not an isolated incident. There are more accounts of the same phenomenon, equally as tragic. Somehow *friendly fire* feels too kind a phrase to describe this horror.

The official term for friendly fire is *fratricide,* the killing of one's brother or sister. A less well known term for this tragedy is *amicide,* which means specifically the killing of one's friends.

A friend and colleague of mine, Chuck Stecker, who recently retired as a lieutenant colonel in the army, shared a great deal with me on the topic of friendly fire. He mused over how the effects of fratricide can be devastating and spread deeply within a unit. It increases the risk of unacceptable losses and the risk of mission failure. It affects the unit's ability to survive and function. He recalled these observations made by units that had experienced friendly fire:

- Hesitation to conduct limited-visibility operations

- Loss of confidence in the unit's leadership

- Increase of leader self-doubt

- Oversupervision of units

- Loss of initiative

- Loss of aggressiveness during combat

- Disrupted operations

- Needless loss of combat power

- General degradation of cohesion and morale

As I have read numerous recollections of friendly fire, I have found a thread of similar emotions woven through each story. There are feelings of anger, doubt, resentment, guilt, fear, and lack of trust, to name a few. Put yourself in a pair of combat boots for a minute. You've been in the desert for weeks now. You're baking in the heat. Your mouth is parched worse than it's ever been in any athletic competition. Every muscle is sore from the awkward maneuvers you've put your body through in the last few days. Your head aches from a combination of squinting up into the scorching sun and the tension of being in the middle of a battle with real guns, real bullets, and real grenades. Worst of all, you've had to encounter real death—the death of your comrades.

There's a lot on your mind as you crouch ever-expectantly in that makeshift bunker. But you mustn't allow your mind to be crowded with nonessential thoughts. This is war, and all concentration is to be focused on the battle. But try as you may, you just can't get that friendly fire incident out of your mind. Your eyes well up with tears as you think of your friend Charlie. While he was still alive he was such a cut-up. He was always grousing about the lousy food. He bragged so much about his wife back home, everyone concluded he must have married a beauty-contest winner who was using her award money to study brain surgery. And his little boy, Kyle . . . Charlie was one proud father. Everyone in the unit knew the smile of the gregarious three-year-old blond, thanks to the tiny, wallet-sized photo Charlie treasured.

So why did he have to take one in the back from one of our own guys? It's the question that hits first and lingers longest. The question gnaws away at any attempt at logic or sense. As your mind dwells on this injustice, more emotions set in.

5

Why am I alive? you ask yourself as guilt starts to play with your mind. *It should've been me. Charlie had so much back home to live for. I'm sitting here complaining that my muscles ache and poor Charlie is dead! It would've made better sense in the grand scheme of things for the bullet to hit someone else—like me.*

Fear is attached to guilt's coattails. *Maybe the friendly fire isn't over yet,* you conclude nervously. *Maybe I'm the next guy on its victims list.* With that chilling thought your body literally shudders, quite an irony in the desert heat. *What if I get shot from behind?*

In fear's wake is anger and resentment. *Why am I even here?* you think as your teeth clench and your hand instinctively tightens its grip on your rifle. *Somebody else should be here in my place. I'm not a big believer in war, anyway. I'm not the right guy for this job. Get someone else.* As you speak to yourself you realize it is just that, words to yourself. No one is there to make your situation any less stressful. You spit in the sand in total anger and disgust. Friendly fire has intensified your situation.

What follows is the saddest commentary of all. Your eyes dart around at all the other soldiers in your bunker. But as you stare at them, it's not with eyes of camaraderie but eyes of distrust. *Which one of you is gonna take a shot at me?* you think to yourself as your glance turns to a steely glare of hate. Hesitation has set in. Because of fear you are unable to move, and in that flash of uncertainty, valuable seconds are lost that can mean the difference between life and death. Your woeful conclusion is *I'm not gonna trust anybody out here—not even my fellow soldiers.*

In all the conversations I have had with military personnel and in the numerous articles and publications I have read on friendly fire, there is remarkable consistency concerning the proposed solutions. While some propose mammoth budgets and research in order to develop elaborate technology and programs, the majority believe that the solutions to the problem of friendly fire are human rather than mechanical or technological. They talk about an emphasis on:

- *increased training,* including the ability to identify the uniforms of friend or foe,

- *conditioning,* because fatigue can lead to costly mistakes,

- *discipline,* giving the ability to maintain control and some semblance of calm even in the midst of the organized chaos of battle, and

- *keeping the troops informed.* Communication helps to instill confidence in leadership and security in what is going to take place.

Friendly Fire in the Church

Regrettably, what is happening on the battlefield is also occurring in Christ's body, the church. Friendly fire is a reality that many Christians are choosing to ignore, but in doing so, they are allowing a natural attrition that is staggering. We cannot and should not have to tolerate this sort of casualty. Nevertheless, the situation persists, especially in the American church.

The identical scenario described above is taking place in the hearts of good Christians everywhere. Questions abound in this vein:

- *Who is on my side?*

- *Who is my enemy?*

- *Why am I here?*

- *Whom can I trust?*

- *Why is this battle important, anyway?*

- *Is my friend's grenade going to end up in my foxhole?*

Friendly fire usually occurs in battle due to one of two possible reasons: (1) technical error, or (2) human error. Sadly, within the church it is not a matter of technical error but a matter of *human choice.* We decide whom we want to attack—even if it's one of our own—and often we go for it with a vengeance. In other words, we have misidentified the enemy.

Imagine the rip-roaring days of the Wild West. Back in the mid to late 1800s the army was often stationed in an uncharted area, literally out in the middle of nowhere, as a means of protection for the pioneers from the enemies of the wilderness. Usually a basic fort was constructed, the type of structure you've seen in dozens of movies. You know the kind I mean—the buildings were surrounded by trunks of tall trees, stripped of all their branches and roped together to look like an early version of a telephone-pole convention. The trees formed a square that protected those within its walls. High up on each corner was the guard post, where a soldier would faithfully look out for the slightest trace of an enemy attack. His alarm would send the troops into battle. We'll call our base of operation *Fort Misidentification.*

But in this imaginary fort there is something dramatically wrong. There is no real interest in the distinct possibility of attack from an outside enemy. No, in Fort Misidentification there is another battle going on, and it's all taking place within the four walls of the fort! No one is shooting over the walls at the real enemy; rather, everyone is shooting at each other. A corporal takes aim at his sergeant while a private has the major in his sights. Rifles are being shot, handguns fired, knives wielded, and, on especially bad days, they actually turn the cannons so they face the inside of the fort, and they fire on each other! The casualties are many because the weapons are real. The soldiers have misidentified the real enemy, and thus they are destroying themselves in the process.

This illustration seems absurd in army life, yet it appropriately describes what is occurring in the church today. The question that begs an answer is *Why?* Why are we working so hard to kill our own troops? What is the basis for this internal destruction?

The Cause of the Kingdom

The answer to that question has its root in what draws people together. Throughout history people have been brought together to both defend and further a cause. The cause may be political, it may be economic, it may be social, it may be religious, or it may be any issue that a philosophy could be built around. But the point is, men and women of all time have been called together around something deemed worth fighting for . . . a cause.

Even a study of church history will demonstrate that the church has rallied around many issues over the centuries. Yet, in retrospect, some seemed insignificant in comparison to others. For Christians of all times and all places, the one cause worth giving their lives for has been the cause of the gospel of God's grace and His kingdom—God's kingdom.

It's not wrong to come together over political issues or social issues or more specific religious issues, but the real cause—the greater cause to champion—is the cause of Christ, that He will build His church and the gates of hell will not be able to withstand it. We must be careful not to call people to an inferior cause. We need to stop championing causes that are divisive to the body; instead we must call people to a unifying cause, which is the proclamation of the gospel and the expansion of the kingdom.

We're in this war together. We're on the same side. Many of us grew up singing a great hymn of our faith, "Onward Christian Soldiers." The lyrics liken the church to a mighty army fighting a spiritual battle. Recently I came across this parody of the hymn by George Verwer:

> Backward Christian soldiers, fleeing from the fight,
> With the cross of Jesus clearly out of sight.
> Christ our rightful Master stands against the foe,
> But forward into battle we are chicken to go!
>
> Like a mighty tortoise moves the church of God,
> Brothers, we are treading where we've often trod.
> We are much divided, many bodies we,
> Having different doctrines, not much charity.
>
> Crowns and thrones may perish, kingdoms rise and wane,
> But the church of Jesus hidden does remain,
> Gates of hell should never 'gainst the church prevail.
> We have Christ's own promise, but think that it will fail.

Sit here, then, ye people, join our useless throng,
Blend with ours your voices in a feeble song.
Blessings, ease, and comfort, ask from Christ the King.
With our modern thinking, we won't do a thing.[2]

Not a very flattering look at our "army" is it? But it's true! We need to develop a unity that springs from the basis of our faith. One of the earliest statements of faith in the history of the church was the Apostles' Creed. This document was developed over the centuries. Although it was not authored by the apostles themselves, it is certainly apostolic in its content. It is representative of the growth and development of the teachings of the early church.

The first creed or formulation of the beliefs of the early church to be officially approved was the Nicene Creed, which was composed at the Council of Nicaea in A.D. 325.

Almost seventeen hundred years later, a group of theologians, pastors, and laypeople authored a series of volumes titled *The Fundamentals*. Published between 1910 and 1915, these booklets defined what had been the non-negotiables of the faith since the Apostles' Creed. In the next chapter we will develop this list with greater detail, but for now, look at these five stalwart issues of our faith:

1. The infallibility of Scripture

2. The deity of Christ

3. The virgin birth and miracles of Christ

4. Christ's substitutionary death

5. Christ's physical resurrection and eventual return[3]

We want to promote agreement based on these five doctrines. When we agree on these issues, we are in agreement toward a larger cause: the cause of the kingdom. But there is a very essential matter of approach that needs to be addressed.

Tasks and Relationships

Since this book is geared primarily to men, I want you to understand an insight I have observed over years in the pastorate and, most recently, at my post in the Promise Keepers organization. It's nothing new or surprising, but it is important: *Men are highly task oriented and not very relationally oriented.* With that amazing statement as context, here's what I see. Since men are task oriented, they want to know what is ahead for them and why. Using the military vernacular, if a man knows what hill he will die on and why, he will boldly march right up to it with great bravery.

Another way to look at it is this: Relationships plus tasks equal increased effectiveness. But tasks without relationships end up with minimal impact. This is because people feel used like pawns in someone else's game of chess without the base of a relationship.

We will cover various tasks as we unfold these truths, but the issue of greater importance is relationships. If we get along with each other, it is the result of embracing shared beliefs within the context of relationship. The New Testament speaks repeatedly of *fellowship.* It is this idea of relationship that will bring us into unity. The church has experienced much growth and progress over the last two thousand years, but it doesn't get real high grades in the relationship department. Dick Halverson, chaplain of the United States Senate, put it in these thought-provoking words:

> In the beginning the church was a fellowship of men and women centering on the living Christ. Then the church moved to Greece where it became a philosophy. Then it moved to Rome where it became an institution. Next, it moved to Europe, where it became a culture. And, finally, it moved to America where it became an enterprise.[4]

To see how this happened, we need to go back to the original intent from the book of Acts. This is what Luke recorded at the end of Peter's sermon at Pentecost:

> Those who accepted his message were baptized, and about three thousand were added to their number that day.

> They devoted themselves to the apostles' teaching and to the fellow-
> ship, to the breaking of bread and to prayer. (Acts 2:41–42)

The early church made a priority out of relating to each other, as is shown a few verses later: "All the believers were together and had everything in common" (Acts 2:44).

The primary focus of the New Testament teaching on unity is not on *organizational* unity. The primary focus is on a *relational* unity that is based upon a foundational set of shared beliefs and the fact that the believers are already one in Christ. As we develop a unity that grows out of relating to one another, we experience such wonderful by-products as love, harmony, and mutual encouragement. Jesus spoke over and over about the love that would characterize our relational unity:

> A new command I give you: Love one another. As I have loved you,
> so you must love one another. By this all men will know that you are my
> disciples, if you love one another. (John 13:34–35)

And Jesus repeated His words two chapters later in John 15:12–13, 17:

> My command is this: Love each other as I have loved you. Greater love
> has no one than this, that he lay down his life for his friends. . . . This
> is my command: Love each other.

Here Jesus described what I would term an *internal* unity. It is a unity that manifests itself through the Spirit. In contrast, *external* unity is an organizational unity within the church that does not come from within. Many of us have resisted a person's attempts to corral us with an external unity made up of rules, regulations, and structures from without. Oftentimes, this imposing of structure may cause issues of disunity to surface. Thus, external unity does not prove that a genuine relational unity exists.

Once we rally around the cause of the gospel and the kingdom, we make great progress toward the internal unity that is so vital to the twentieth-century church. But will that rallying point be sufficient to halt the friendly fire? We need to look at this issue from another angle.

Why Do People Fight?

Folks have been fighting forever. Inborn from our sin nature is this desire to disagree. Everyone has it. Some express it more freely than others, but it's deep down inside all of us. So why do people fight against each other? Primarily, people fight to *validate their own existence.*

A person feels more important, more valuable, of greater worth, if he fights for his position and wins. It's the oldest game in the book—a game of power, prestige, and position. My friend Dr. Rod Cooper (a contributor to this book) has studied extensively in this field, and he has concluded that the fundamental cause for fights is low self-esteem. Have you ever heard the expression, "I'd like to punch his lights out"? We make our lights shine brighter by dimming all other lights around us. But that's far from a smart battle plan.

Churches can follow the same pattern individuals follow. I've seen this happen more than once, but one of the most vivid examples of disunity among believers came a number of years ago, when I was asked to speak at a church that was in need of a senior pastor. Despite what I considered my most inspired efforts, no job offer was forthcoming. While I didn't understand then why God had closed that door of opportunity to me at the time, it became obvious shortly thereafter.

It wasn't too long after the church's new pastor arrived that things began to get a little rough. We began to hear accusations and counter-accusations concerning how the church was to function and how its ministry was to be carried out.

Various Christian arbitrators were called in but to no avail. Eventually the divided congregation wound up in the courts, and its problems were aired on the front page of the local newspaper. To most people the issues seemed pretty simple. They didn't revolve around core and essential beliefs but rather around styles of dress and worship, organizational structure, and who had access to the checkbook and bank accounts.

While the two sides were awaiting the court's decision, a temporary order was imposed by the judge that essentially split the church building. One part of the congregation could meet in the sanctuary, and the other group (who had called a new pastor for themselves) could meet in another. They continued to fight over who got how many hymnals and which congregation got the newer piano.

By the time the judge had rendered his final decision, all credibility was lost. A church that had once been known for its effective ministries and outreach into the community had become a source of derision and scorn. The community, which had once shown respect, now mocked the church and mocked the God these people said they represented.

Disunity brings shame and reproach to the name and message of Christ. In contrast, the ability to live in the midst of diversity declares that there is a God who is greater than our differences and shows that God can do what man cannot.

Just as these arguing church members did, we fight with others to justify our position. It's not at all what the Bible teaches. The apostle Paul taught the believers in Galatia a model for dealing with disagreement, even if the point of disagreement is sin:

> Brothers, if someone is caught in a sin, you who are spiritual should restore him gently. But watch yourself, or you also may be tempted. (Gal. 6:1)

Certainly there are occasions that call for confrontation and rebuke, but the end result should be restoration and growth, not destruction. Charles Colson, in his excellent book *The Body*, makes this astute observation:

> The less secure people are in their beliefs, the more strident they become. Conversely, the more confident people are of the truth, the more grace they exhibit to those who don't agree.[5]

When I was a pastor, I had an experience that gave me firsthand exposure to this phenomenon. At one particular church I served, there was a suggestion that all the churches in this small town join hands to sponsor a community-wide cooperative event to celebrate this town's religious history. I thought it was a wonderful idea, jumped on board, and worked hard to create an event that would be tasteful, memorable, and full of impact.

What had all the potential to be a marvelous demonstration of internal unity was greatly misunderstood by one pastor in particular. Rather than a manifestation of pure love, he took it upon himself to "purify" his flock from the compromise of such an event. He took to his pulpit weekly, always including words in his sermon directed at me and my willingness to "sell out" by compromising. Cooperating with the likes of all the churches in town could get you a bad reputation!

To further complicate matters, this pastor began to write and distribute letters that were critical of me. It became a bit embarrassing.

What really bothered me most was that this man was not from our town and he had never even talked to me personally about the issues that offended him. He was not applying Galatians 6:1 in the least. This was not about restoring. This was about his perception of an error within me and his manipulating of that error in order to put himself forward at my expense.

By the way, in spite of all this personal trauma, the event itself was a great success with many people in our town being blessed.

The personal incident with the pastor reminded me of an illustration I first heard Steve Brown use on his radio broadcast. He explained that when a group of thoroughbred horses face attack from an outside enemy, they stand in a circle facing each other and, with their back legs, kick out at the enemy. Donkeys, on the other hand, do just the opposite. They circle up, facing the enemy, and use their hind legs to kick each other! How often does the church do the identical thing—ignore the real enemy while we are attacking fellow believers?

It's time to call a cease-fire in this war within our own borders. Each person, myself included, needs to ask himself the question, *Who am I lobbing grenades at?* Am I focusing on the enemy, or am I attacking my own brother? Unity is essential in gaining a victory against our real enemy,

Satan. I like the inspiring words of the former chairman of the Joint Chiefs of Staff, General Colin L. Powell, as he spoke to the issue of military unity:

> When a team takes to the field, individual specialists come together to achieve a team win. All players try to do their very best because every other player, the team, and the hometown are counting on them to win.
>
> So it is when the Armed Forces of the United States go to war. We must win every time.
>
> Every soldier must take the battlefield believing his or her unit is the best in the world.
>
> Every pilot must take off believing there is no one better in the sky.
>
> Every sailor standing watch must believe there is no better ship at sea.
>
> Every marine must hit the beach believing that there are no better infantrymen in the world.
>
> But they all must believe that they are part of a team, a joint team, that fights together to win.
>
> This is our history, this is our tradition, this is our future.[6]

Conclusion

Although this entire chapter has been built around the metaphor of friendly fire, let me again remind you of a key distinction between the illustration and the truth. Fighting within the body of Christ is *always by human choice,* not by any technical error. This is a plea to consciously choose not to fight, but to love our brothers in the unity Christ intended for us to exhibit. It's the only way we can be effective witnesses for Christ and the gospel. Choosing to love does not bypass the biblical mandate of dealing with perceived error but rather defines the attitude, atmosphere, and means by which differences will be handled.

Friendly fire isn't a pretty picture, is it? In fact, the term itself leaves me with a sick feeling in the pit of my stomach. So let's get together, start lobbing grenades in the right direction, and get on with the fighting of battles and being the church. Right?

Well, not so fast. Remember we stated that one of the primary issues in minimizing friendly fire was training in the ability to correctly identify the enemy. We want the ability to discern friend from foe, even in the midst of battle, and then to act accordingly.

The next two chapters will deal with some of the additional training we need. First, what is the unity Jesus prayed for in John 13 and 17? Who do I invite into the foxhole with me? And second, what is the foundation of unity? Is there a core set of beliefs that must be shared?

Recently I read the writing of an American historian who made a passing comment on our nation's battle for independence. He estimated that if all the American colonies had been more unified at the time of the American Revolution, we could have won our war for independence in *one year!* Instead, because of division, it took eight times that long . . . eight bloody years of hard-fought battle.

Let's take a cue from a two-hundred-year-old mistake. Let's unite and fight the good fight together.

Personal Evaluation

Read each of the following statements and rate yourself on a scale from 1 to 10, with 1 being "I totally disagree" and 10 being "I totally agree."

_____ 1. Friendly fire is a major problem facing the church today.

_____ 2. I have done more to contribute to unity than diversity.

_____ 3. There is only one cause to rally around, and that is the cause of the kingdom of Christ.

_____ 4. The essentials of our faith are those five areas listed on page 10.

_____ 5. I fight in order to validate my own existence.

_____ 6. I am more task oriented than relationally oriented.

_____ 7. I demonstrate the unity Christ spoke of by loving my brothers.

In the Group

This book is designed to stimulate discussion between men. If you are not already in a small group, take this opportunity to form one.

Look for men who are willing to be more open and vulnerable than usual. You can make it as homogeneous or as diverse as you wish.

1. If this is your first time together as a group, take a few minutes to become acquainted with each other. Start by describing the three most memorable experiences in your life (in three minutes or less!).

2. What are you hoping to gain by being in this group? Share some of these goals with the group.

3. How would you describe your relationship to Jesus Christ? Can you articulate where you are spiritually? Give it a try!

4. Without naming names, can you share a story of friendly fire in the church? How were you affected by this incident?

5. What do you think you personally can do to begin bringing about unity in Christ's body?

6. Go around the group and have each person share one request for the others to remember in prayer. Close your session by praying together. Thank the Lord for His church, which He has purchased. Perhaps you'd like to pick a partner who will pray for you specifically all throughout this study time together. If that is the case, break off in groups of two for a time of prayer.

Memory Verse: "A new command I give you: Love one another. As I have loved you, so you must love one another. By this all men will know that you are my disciples, if you love one another" (John 13:34–35).

Chapter Two

That They May Be One

OKAY, I'LL ADMIT IT. I tend to push myself harder than I should. In many ways, I am like many American men. I'm a hard driver, a busy man, a mover/shaker—whatever you want to call it. Let's just say it takes a lot to keep me down.

And that's exactly what happened this past summer . . . *a lot* happened to keep me down. The timing was horrible, from a human perspective. I was jetting all over the country, developing new areas, and speaking for Promise Keepers—and enjoying every ministry minute of it. We had almost finished the conference season. I had spoken at a number of events called Wake Up Calls, designed to challenge men and excite them about their place in this world. They were smaller versions of the stadium rallies we were presenting across the United States. It was right in the middle of this exhilarating time that my schedule suddenly lurched to a screeching halt. I felt severe chest pains while I was participating in one of our conferences and was immediately rushed to the hospital.

I thought I had had a heart attack.

Actually, it turned out to be less serious. The physician described it as an artery that went into spasms, but the symptoms were quite similar to a heart attack. Sitting in a hospital bed for four days and wondering about the outcome of all the tests tends to get a guy's attention—even a guy like me who keeps busy, has important things to do, and is hard driving.

Susan was understandably concerned. She leaned over the bed, squeezed my hand, and said, "You've been speaking at Wake Up Calls all over the country. God just gave you yours."

It's a sobering feeling to hear your kids whisper to their mom, "Is Daddy gonna die?" Susan reassured them as best she could, but there was no denying the fact that this was something to be treated seriously.

I was fortunate to be able to recover so thoroughly. During that recovery I did some careful reflection and made some necessary changes in my lifestyle. God had spared me and scared me, and for that, I was grateful.

Yet, after the hospital stay, I noticed how hard it was for me to get up and get going in the morning. It was difficult for me to get motivated, largely because I knew my body wasn't quite up to speed. There was pain, something I had not felt before.

Why does one part of my body have such an effect on all the rest of it? I would think to myself. *Why do I feel like my eyes don't focus as well as they used to? Why do my feet feel so heavy, and why does my concentration tend to wander? I should feel a little discomfort in my chest and that's it, right?*

Wrong.

When one part of the body doesn't function properly, every part is affected. Stub your toe . . . your whole body reacts. Hit your finger with a hammer . . . the pain doesn't just stay in your hand. Blow out your knee in a sports contest, and you are in agony from the top of your head to the soles of your feet.

I have always found this concept particularly amazing in the world of professional sports. And I imagine there is no finer illustration of the workings of the body than a professional football player in the National Football League. Those guys are truly iron men. I've had occasion to wander around the training facilities of a few of the teams, and the weightrooms are incredible! The men of the NFL specialize in maximizing all the strength their bodies can muster. I'll admit, when I see the huge weights piled on the bars for their three sets of ten-rep bench presses, I wonder if I could even do it with the bare bar!

So take this finely tuned machine—the body of a National Football League player—and add one more ingredient, and you'll see what I am driving at. What happens when one of these players is injured? That's right; all the practice and training and effort are overshadowed by the fact that part of the player's body is unable to function as it was intended.

Most of us understand this principle when we see a horrible injury on the field. A broken leg, a concussion, a dislocated shoulder, a sprained knee—all are injuries that can sideline a player for an extended period of time. Yet to be honest, there are some injuries I've never quite understood. I think the one that intrigues me the most is when you hear a guy say on the pregame show: "So-and-So will not be able to play today. He's on the sideline nursing a bad case of *turf toe!*"

It makes me laugh just to think about it. Here's a guy who can bench-press North Dakota. He runs the forty in 4.5 seconds. Last week he couldn't be stopped, even when he was double-teamed and triple-teamed by the opposition. Now he's on the sideline because he hurt his *big toe!*

Take, for example, Mark Bavarro, the fine tight end for the Philadelphia Eagles. His turf toe was so painful it caused him to miss three or four games in a row! And then there's Bill Bates, defensive and special-teams specialist for the Dallas Cowboys. In his autobiography *Shoot for the Star,* he writes about how he suffered with turf toe off and on for four seasons! From 1989 to 1992 he often found it necessary to take anti-inflammatory medicines just to bring his turf toe under enough control so he could play. And anyone who knows Bill Bates knows this is a man with an extraordinary threshold for pain. He seems to have played in pain every week for twelve years now.

The truth is, of course, you need your toes to gain thrust. In order to tap into the speed a player has developed, he needs the use of his feet and toes to push off the ground. When artificial surfaces were introduced, it was quickly learned that their main disadvantage is that they do not "give" like natural surfaces. The cleats worn on the artificial surface can't dig into the ground; thus it's easy to inflame the area around the bones in the big toe and ball of the foot on Astroturf (thus the name turf toe).

So, as funny as it sounds, it is not uncommon for a player to be sidelined because of turf toe; a perfectly conditioned human being in every way, forced to sit out of an athletic competition because one tiny part of his body is unable to cooperate.

What is true for every human body is likewise true for Christ's body, the church. Every part of His body is affected by the actions of one part. If your leg is in a cast, it's going to have an impact on your whole body. If we can keep all the parts of the body functioning the way God intended them, we can truly experience the sort of relationship with each other that brings glory to Him. That's why unity is so important, now more than ever.

It seems that no matter where I go I am being asked about this thing called "unity in the body." Some people say we simply need to skip ahead to what we believe. While I commend them for their zeal, I fully realize that all within the body of Christ come from a variety of backgrounds. It is out of these backgrounds that I have both read and listened to multiple descriptions and definitions all seeking to define what Jesus meant when He spoke of the power and effect that his kind of unity would have on this world. It is vitally important, therefore, that we understand what He meant by what He said if we are going to experience the *Awesome Power of Shared Beliefs*.

Unity: What It Isn't

Since we're trying to establish a case for biblical unity, it might be helpful to first distinguish what is *not* meant by the use of the term. Perhaps this contrast will further highlight the truth. First of all, unity is not a oneness at the expense of the truth. Unity is not an ecumenical endeavor to find the lowest common denominator among people even if it means denying cardinal doctrines such as the deity of Christ or the inerrancy of the Scriptures. As you read on, you will see that we won't sacrifice the truth, but actually we will use it as the foundation for the oneness we so earnestly seek.

Second, unity is not a political organization. There is no hidden agenda serving as the underpinnings of unity. Oneness isn't a front for a slick way of bilking people of their money, time, and resources. It just doesn't work that way in Christ's body.

Third, unity is not something you can develop or enhance through a program or a curriculum. You could never have enough boards and committees to stimulate or maintain it.

Finally, unity is not an ecclesiastical organization. At first blush that statement may surprise you, but the meaning is understood by contrasting the words *organization* and *organism*. As was developed in the last chapter, the unity spoken of by the Scripture is *relational* and is based on a set of core beliefs. It's not an external thing such as we see in so many organizations, but it is alive—a real, breathing, heart-beating, fully functioning organism! It's a body, not a building!

In what has become one of my favorite "Peanuts" cartoons, Lucy demands that Linus change TV channels and then threatens him with her fist if he doesn't cooperate with her request immediately.

"What makes you think you can walk right in here and take over?" Linus asks quizzically.

"These five fingers," Lucy says. "Individually they are nothing, but when I curl them together like this into a single unit, they form a weapon that is terrible to behold!"

"Which channel do you want?" Linus asks, thoroughly dejected, as Lucy smiles victoriously.

Turning away, he looks at his fingers and says, "Why can't you guys get organized like that?"[1]

That kind of unity comes from the oneness of an *organism*. All those fingers have something no organization can boast of. They are related to one another by the fact that they are all part of the hand. No committee, club, or group can make that claim, and therein lies the key to biblical unity.

Unity: What It Is

What is unity? It is being in relationship to one another.

This is a unity rooted in love, sacrifice, and a common commitment to Jesus Christ. As Christians we are to prefer another over ourselves. We need a spiritual unity like this to transcend even our political activist rhetoric—a unity that can contribute to the spiritual revival we so desperately desire and need.

Relationship brings about so much of the practical applications of the Scriptures. Through relating to one another we are able to offer such things as

- encouragement,

- support,

- correction,

- fellowship,

- love, and

- increased effectiveness.

It's noteworthy to observe that nowhere does Jesus teach about organization. It is not until the Epistles that we are taught about organizational structure within the body, and that instruction is somewhat limited. Even there the emphasis is relational. The Lord Jesus made statements like this one, recorded by Matthew in his account of the gospel: "And on this rock I will build my church, and the gates of Hades will not overcome it" (Matt. 16:18b).

The lesson is expanded in Christ's prayer recorded in John 17. Commentators have called this prayer many things throughout the years, but I prefer to think of it as Christ's prayer, His heart, for our unity. At the conclusion of the prayer, He stated:

> My prayer is not for them alone. I pray also for those who will believe in me through their message, that all of them may be one, Father, just as you are in me and I am in you. May they also be in us so that the world may believe that you have sent me. . . . I in them and you in me. May they be brought to complete unity to let the world know that you sent me and have loved them even as you have loved me. . . .

Righteous Father, though the world does not know you, I know you, and they know that you have sent me. I have made you known to them, and will continue to make you known in order that the love you have for me may be in them and that I myself may be in them. (John 17:20–21, 23, 25–26)

What is particularly amazing to me about this prayer for unity is that Christ uses the Godhead as His illustration of how unity works. The Father, the Son, and the Holy Spirit are all in relationship with each other. They are the Three in One. Both unity and diversity are emphasized by the reference to the Trinity. God has modeled His request for us.

Also within this passage is the indisputable truth that the unity sought is a *spiritual* unity. William Hendriksen put it this way:

> The unity for which Jesus is praying is not merely outward. He guards against this very common misinterpretation. He asks that the oneness of all believers resemble that which exists eternally between the Father and the Son. In both cases the unity is of a definitely *spiritual* nature. To be sure, Father, Son, and Holy Spirit are one *in essence*; believers, on the other hand, are one in mind, effort and purpose. . . .
>
> When believers are united in the faith and present a common front to the world, they exert power and influence. When they are torn asunder by strife and dissension, the world will not know what to make of them, nor how to interpret their so-called "testimonies." Believers, therefore, should always yearn for peace, but never for peace at the expense of truth, for unity which has been gained by means of such a sacrifice is not worthy of the name.[2]

In his commentary on the Gospel of John, Leon Morris agrees, and he makes the following observation:

> The unity for which He prays is to lead to a fuller experience of the Father and the Son. And this, in turn, will have the further consequences that the world will believe. . . .
>
> It will transcend all human unity. The unity in question, while it is a spiritual unity, rather than one of organization, as we have seen, yet has an outward expression, for it is a unity which the world can observe and which will influence the world.[3]

So, putting the teaching altogether from this passage and others, a model for unity can be identified and understood.

A Model of Unity

The New Testament offers a wonderful glimpse at what unity looks like. John 17 teaches us first of all the *pattern* for unity, which is the Godhead. The requests that we demonstrate unity, fellowship, and love are generously modeled by the Trinity. Colson reminds us how brilliant this analogy is, especially to today's world:

> The unity of the church expressed in our Lord's prayer in John 17 is not the kind of unity that is being touted by the World Council of Churches. They have tried to reduce the elements of faith to the lowest common denominator. . . .
>
> True unity is not sought by pretending that there are no differences, as modern ecumenists have done, but by recognizing and respecting those differences, while focusing on the great orthodox truths all Christians share.[4]

Not only do we see the pattern of unity in this passage, but we also see unity's *purpose*. The reason for unity is stated in John 17:21—"that the world may believe." Unity results in greater effectiveness in ministry. One needs only to look around at all the Christians bickering with each other today to realize that the small effectiveness of the church is in direct relation to the extent to which the church is functioning in unity. Perhaps the following parable can express this truth more effectively:

> The wedding guests have gathered in great anticipation; the ceremony to be performed today has been long awaited. The orchestra begins to play an anthem, and the choir rises in proper precision. The Bridegroom and his attendants gather in front of the chancel. One little saint, her flowering hat bobbing, leans to her companion and whispers, "Isn't he handsome?" The response is agreement. "My, yes. The handsomest."
>
> One by one, the bridesmaids, heralds of the nuptials, begin to stride in measured patterns. Several flower girls sow rose petals upon the white, unmarked aisle cloth. The sound of the organ rises, a joyous announce-

ment that the bride is coming. Everyone stands and strains to get a proper glimpse of the beauty—then a horrible gasp explodes from the congregation. This is a bride like no other.

In she stumbles—something terrible has happened! One leg is twisted; she limps pronouncedly. The wedding garment is tattered and muddy; great rents in the dress leave her scarcely modest. Black bruises can be seen welting her bare arms; the bride's nose is bloody. An eye is swollen, yellow and purple in its discoloration. Patches of hair look as if they had actually been pulled from her scalp.

Fumbling over the keys, the organist begins again after his shocked pause. The attendants cast their eyes down. The congregation mourns silently. Surely the Bridegroom deserved better than this! That handsome Prince who has kept himself faithful to his love should find consummation with the most beautiful of women—not this.

His bride, the church, has been fighting again.[5]

Could it be that the church in the United States is barely keeping up with the population growth because of a lack of unity? Could our lack of unity be contributing to the moral decline we are experiencing? Even with all that is at our disposal—brilliant theologians, gifted communicators, beautiful facilities, high technology—all the conferences, retreats, and seminars—we're just not making a dent.

We're not transforming the culture. The culture is transforming us. It's time to reverse that trend. That is unity's purpose.

This unity also brings with it a *power*. It is the power that is spoken of in Acts 1:

But you will receive power when the Holy Spirit comes on you; and you will be my witnesses in Jerusalem, and in all Judea and Samaria, and to the ends of the earth. (Acts 1:8)

This is not a political power that we see foretold. Rather, it is a spiritual power—the power to live a godly life in order to influence the world. And this is what was to be . . . the mobilization of an army with a common pattern and purpose, and an awesome power.

If you take a few moments to read the first six chapters of the book of Acts, you will see the fulfillment of Christ's prayer in John 17. Nothing less than explosive growth occurs in those chapters.

But Christ's prayer was not to be considered completely answered in the first century. It is still in effect for us as well. That's part of what makes this passage so exciting. When Jesus prayed in John 17, He was praying for all people of all time, including *you* and *me!*

Conclusion

The story is told of a beautiful little girl who wandered out one cold day into the countryside of Canada. When the appointed time for the little girl's return came and went, her parents eventually concluded that she was lost and gathered the townspeople together to search for her. Fortunately, the town was filled with good people who put their personal concerns aside and began to hunt for the missing little girl. Yet in all their zeal and concern, each townsperson elected to go his or her own way with no apparent regard to what anyone else in the town might be doing.

Ultimately, it became dark and the townspeople reassembled at the home of the lost child. As the cold of the Canadian winter set in on that blustery night, a young man made a suggestion. "Why don't we all join hands and search the large grassy fields near here. With all of us together, we can certainly cover that much land."

The idea was a good one. It wasn't long before this method yielded its result. They found the girl in one of those fields, curled up in a ball. But it was too late. She had been exposed to the frigid winter elements too long, and she had died as a result.

It was at her funeral that the townspeople all seemed to express the same emotion. After paying their respects to her parents, many of them could be seen huddled together in small groups, heads hanging and whispering, *"If only we had joined hands earlier!"*

My concern is that Christ's body function as it was designed to do. It takes all of us. We can't afford to have even one laid up in the hospital. If one part isn't functioning properly, it will affect us all. Promise with me to be a man committed to unity.

One of the most beautiful descriptions of unity is found in the three verses that make up Psalm 133, penned by the shepherd boy who became king—David. Allow its powerful imagery to speak to you as we focus on its message to men and women of all time:

> How good and pleasant it is
>> when brothers live together in unity!
> It is like precious oil poured on the head,
>> running down on the beard,
> running down on Aaron's beard,
>> down upon the collar of his robes.
> It is as if the dew of Hermon
>> were falling on Mount Zion.
> For there the Lord bestows his blessing,
>> Even life forevermore.

Personal Evaluation

Read the following statements and respond to each one of them as honestly as possible:

1. Can you think of one or two of your Christian brothers who make it difficult for you to practice unity?

   _____

   _____

2. Why do these people bother you? Is it something you can look beyond for the sake of unity?

   _____

   _____

   _____

   _____

3. Do you think *you* could be the reason someone else is struggling with unity? What changes can you make in order to make his or her quest a little easier?

_____

_____

_____

_____

4. What is the most important issue you learned while reading this chapter? How will it make a difference in the way you live your life?

_____

_____

_____

_____

In the Group

Now that your group has had a session together, let's see if we can probe a little further into the issue of unity. Remember, don't force anyone to talk, yet make sure everyone who wishes to speak has the opportunity.

1. A fascinating way to get to know each other a little better is to use the analogy of a human body and answer the question, "What part of the body are you?" Be sure to explain your answer.

2. In John 17, Christ prays for our unity, fellowship, and love. Take each of those terms one by one and talk about what it really means to you. Try to be as practical as possible.

3. Why is it difficult for men to be in relationship with each other? Do you think a task-oriented approach to life is an asset or a liability?

4. In your own words, tell the others why you believe unity will cause us to be more effective in ministering to the world around us.

5. The Holy Spirit empowers us to experience the unity Scripture commands. What comes to mind when you think of the word *power*? How can this power be used in a positive way in our witness?

6. As we did last session, let's close our time with prayer. Check in with your partner to see how his week went. Follow up on the requests you've prayed for in his life. Ask about any new requests, then bring him up to date with your situation.

Memory Verse: "My prayer is not for them alone. I pray also for those who will believe in me through their message, that all of them may be one, Father, just as you are in me and I am in you. May they also be in us so that the world may believe that you have sent me" (John 17:20–21).

ChapterThree

The Faith Once for All Entrusted

It was a beautiful church.

I mean the church building. It was the kind of edifice you'd see in an old Norman Rockwell painting. The sanctuary was the kind of room warmed by the deep hues of the woodwork. The pews were the sort with the red pads on the seats. They were old, but they maintained their inviting color. The cross on the front wall called all to worship. It was plain, without flair, but there was just something about it that reminded those attending of why they were there in the first place. The pulpit was just the right size . . . big enough to serve its purpose, but not so large to be overpowering to its audience.

And, of course, the pinnacle of the church's beauty was its breathtaking cavalcade of stained-glass windows. Eight glorious scenes from the Scriptures were portrayed—one in each of the eight windows that bathed the room with the light from above. Four on each side of you as you'd sit in awesome splendor. It was a church building with grace and charm.

But, like any building its age, things had started to deteriorate. The church had to vote to approve some extra funds so that the many leaks in the roof could be repaired. Then the furnace went on the fritz, and the board decided to replace it with a new heater/air-conditioning unit. When the organ starting sounding like the merry-go-round at the carnival, it seemed the right time to purchase a newer, more upscale model.

Yet the greatest concern for this modest congregation came when, for some unexplained reason, the beautiful stained-glass windows started to fall out of the positions they had occupied for years. Carefully, one by one, piece by piece, the magnificent art was returned to its original position. It wasn't long before the church was completely refurbished. It was even more magnificent and inviting than it had been before.

All appeared well for this church, both the building and the people. There was no reason for alarm until one day, not too long after the refurbishing project was completed, something happened . . .

Another portion of a stained-glass window fell from the west wall and tumbled to the ground.

It was at this point that a group of experts in building construction were summoned to investigate the case of the falling windows. They didn't hunt too long before they found their culprit. It was not good news, not good at all. What was the problem here?

The foundation.

Someone had made a bad decision on where to locate this historic church. The building was resting on a bed of sandstone, and its foundation was poorly constructed. All the refurbishing in the world would not rescue this building from its more serious dilemma. The building was atop a weak foundation, and no amount of patching the roof or replacing the furnace or adding a new organ was going to solve the root reason for the falling windows. Even a nonbuilder knows the basic rule—the foundation is essential to the strength of the building. And just as the foundation is essential, so it is that the essentials are the foundation for the unit of our faith.

What we are talking about is *doctrine.* I once read a brochure for a local church that stated, "Since love unites and doctrine divides, our church concentrates on love." What was ironic about the brochure was that on the back it had printed the congregation's statement of faith!

What they couldn't see was that sound doctrine does in fact divide, but it also unites. It is sound doctrine that enables us to love what is true and hate what is false. It is sound doctrine that enables us to live lives that are pleasing to God. It is sound doctrine that draws the body of Christ together and confronts error.

For instance, I have a friend who doesn't believe that we are saved by grace through faith. He believes people get to heaven on the basis of their good works, but since the standard is so high, why bother?

Here is where sound doctrine divides. The truth of the Scriptures is that our works don't save us (see Eph. 2:8–9). Sound doctrine says my friend is not a Christian. Is this harsh? By no means. It helps to clarify how I can help him. He needs sound doctrine. He needs the truth.

Doctrine is the truth that brings us together in the battle we wage against our enemy, the devil. Doctrine is a unifier, even in the military. Here are a few soldiers' comments on the importance of military "doctrine":

> At the very heart of war lies doctrine. It represents the central beliefs for waging war in order to achieve victory. . . . It is the building material for strategy.
> It is fundamental for sound judgment.
> > General Curtis E. LeMay, U. S. Air Force

> Doctrine provides a military organization with a common philosophy, a common language, a common purpose, and a unity of effort.
> > General George H. Decker, U. S. Army

> Doctrine [is] every action that contributes to unity of purpose. . . . It is what warriors believe in and act on.
> > Captain Wayne P. Hughes Jr., U. S. Navy Fleet Tactics

> Doctrine establishes a particular way of thinking about war and a way of fighting. . . . Doctrine provides the basis for harmonious actions and mutual understanding.
> > Fleet Marine Force Manual 1, Warfighting[1]

The apostle Paul made a similar statement about the importance of doctrine when he said, "Watch your life and doctrine closely. Persevere in them, because if you do, you will save both yourself and your hearers" (1 Tim. 4:16).

This chapter is not about bringing down walls that divide us as much as it is about building a foundation to support us. In order to realize the awesome power of shared beliefs as our Lord intended, we must embrace the *right* beliefs. We must realize there is also an awesome power in sharing *wrong* belief systems. One doesn't have to look too far back in history to see the incredible power for evil that the shared belief systems in places like Nazi Germany and Cambodia have had. We saw it in our own country in the years of slavery that were perpetuated by a shared belief system that held to a less-than-human concept of the non-white races. What tremendous pain has been unleashed upon mankind around the globe, all in the name of a "shared belief" system!

It is imperative that the body of Christ come together around a true set of core beliefs if we are to have a positive impact on this world. This impact will occur because the beliefs are good and God will bless us. What are the essentials of the faith upon which we can stand and upon which we can unite? What are these common truths that will bring an end to the needless friendly fire? What common ground will bring the body of Christ into the unity for which Christ prayed? Let's look more closely at these doctrines in order to be better prepared for the war that surrounds us.

The Essentials of the Faith

In order to ascertain what is the foundation upon which the church is built, it would be wise to take a look at what was considered important to the body earlier in its history. For example, in the last half of the second century, the church was being bothered by the false teachings of two different heresies, Gnosticism and Montanism. The former taught that Christ never came to earth in human form, and the latter contended that the Holy Spirit didn't arrive at Pentecost but was coming soon and, along with Him, the end of the world. Both of these were in need of addressing.

Since both of these teachings were absolutely contradictory to the truth of God's Word, the church fathers put together a statement of belief that summarized what the apostles had taught concerning the faith. We know this statement today as the Apostles' Creed. It states the following truths:

> I believe in God, the Father almighty, creator of heaven and earth, and in Jesus Christ, His only begotten Son, our Lord, who was conceived by the Holy Spirit, born of the virgin Mary, suffered under Pontius Pilate, was crucified, died, and was buried; He descended into hell; on the third day He rose again from the dead; He ascended into heaven, and sitteth at the right hand of God the Father almighty; from thence He shall come to judge the quick and the dead.
>
> I believe in the Holy Spirit, the holy Christian church, the communion of saints, the forgiveness of sins, the resurrection of the body, and the life everlasting. Amen.

We don't know the author of that document, but for centuries it has been viewed as an acceptable summation of what the apostles taught. It is a splendid work, yet marvelously simple.

By the year A.D. 325 more heresy was brewing. This time a man named Arius was teaching that Christ was not as truly and fully God as the Father. Arius called Christ the first and highest of all created beings. As a result, Constantine the Great called for a meeting to settle the dispute. The council took place forty-five miles from Constantinople in a small town called Nicaea. More than a hundred bishops attended, many of them scarred by the tortures they had received in persecution for their faith. They rebuked the teaching of Arius and authored an important document we know as the Nicene Creed. The refined document reads as follows:

> We believe in one God, the Father almighty, maker of all things, both visible and invisible; and in one Lord, Jesus Christ, the son of God, only begotten of the Father, that is to say, of the substance of the Father, God of God and Light of Light, very God of very God, begotten, not made, being of one substance with the Father, by whom all things were made, both things in heaven and things on earth; who, for us men and for our salvation, came down and was made flesh, was made man, suffered, and rose again on the third day, went up into the heavens, and is to come again to judge both the quick and the dead; and in the Holy Ghost.

These documents give us a glimpse into the battle fought in the first two centuries of the church's history. Jim Petersen, in his book *Church without Walls,* gives us insight into these writings:

> What were the defenses against all of these false teachings? One early bulwark was found in the creeds. As the creeds were developed, they served as a plumb line that measured truth against error. The earliest of these, the Apostles' Creed, is of uncertain origin, but it is believed to come from the oral teachings of the apostles and was in common use by the middle of the second century as a confession at baptism. The statement embraced the nature of God, of Jesus Christ, and the essential truths that comprise the gospel.
>
> The Nicene Creed deals with questions concerning the nature of the Incarnation. The phrase "being of one substance with the Father," a part of the creed, reveals the issue that was at stake.
>
> With our reliance on the Scriptures today, these creeds and their successors seem unimportant to many of us. But their role in the history of God's people cannot be underestimated.[2]

In my view all that is necessary to add to the Apostles' Creed and the Nicene Creed is the issue of the inerrancy of Scripture. And I add that only because it was not an issue back then as it is today. The early church fathers accepted the Scriptures as inerrant. We do too.

Staying strong in your beliefs should contribute to unity, not take away from it. Perhaps the key Scripture passage that was written to unify us is Jude 3. This verse has been wrangled around by so many for so long that it is often the motto for much destruction.

Contending versus Contentious

In the next to the last book of the New Testament, we are introduced to a man named Jude, who is the author of the tiny letter. This is not the apostle Jude but rather one of the Lord Jesus' half-brothers. He is called Judas in Matthew 13:55 and Mark 6:3. He had another brother, James, who wrote the Epistle that bears that same name and was also the leader of the Jerusalem church, as seen in Acts 15:13–21.

Jude's letter is intended to serve as a warning against false teachers spreading heresy among the believers. He uses historical illustrations such as unbelieving Israel, disobedient angels, and Sodom and Gomorrah as examples of the Lord's dealings with apostasy. He encourages Christians to deal with this challenge and not be caught off guard.

Specifically, Jude administers a strong admonition to believers of the first century and for today as well:

> Dear friends, although I was very eager to write to you about the salvation we share, I felt I had to write and urge you to contend for the faith that was once for all entrusted to the saints. For certain men whose condemnation was written about long ago have secretly slipped in among you. They are godless men, who change the grace of our God into a license for immorality and deny Jesus Christ our only Sovereign and Lord. (Jude 3–4)

Let's examine what Jude is saying here as he pleads with us not to leave the core set of beliefs to which we adhere.

First of all, what is "the faith" for which we are to contend? Notice the verse says it was "entrusted" to the saints. God has given the faith to us. The facts of the Christian faith were not self-discovered but rather God-revealed. They come from Him, not me.

The faith was also entrusted "once for all." There is an unchangeable and eternal quality about the faith. It is the permanent center or, if you will, the nucleus of Christianity.

Therefore, the faith is the body of truth that took on a definite form early in the history of the church. It is what the apostles taught from the earliest chapters of the book of Acts. That is why the Apostles' Creed and Nicene Creed are vital summaries of truth.

Theologian Simon Kistemaker explains the faith in his *New Testament Commentary*:

> What is this faith Jude mentions? In view of the context, we understand the word [faith] to mean the body of Christian beliefs. It is the gospel the apostles proclaimed and therefore is equivalent to the "apostles' teaching" (Acts 2:42). Thus it is not the trust and confidence

that the individual believer has in God, for this is subjective faith. In this passage Jude speaks of Christian doctrine, that is, objective faith.[3]

Jude speaks of the faith in the context of "the salvation we share." Our faith is the gospel, the non-negotiable, grace-oriented salvation by faith. It is the promise of Jesus Christ's return. It is this issue of being saved, not just for now, but for all eternity. This, then, is the core.

The scene is easy to imagine. Jude sits down, all prepared to write a letter to his Christian brothers and sisters about this salvation they all share in common. But due to the entrance of heretical teachings, a departure from the core beliefs, Jude feels no peace about his original intent. No, he needs to change the subject of his letter to a topic of greater urgency. It's as if he is saying, "You know the faith we all share in common? Well stay with it!"

Thus, the next question is, what does it really mean to *contend* for this faith? It is of interest to point out that in the original Greek language, in which this passage is written, the word for *contend* is in a verb form stressing continuous action. The idea of *contending* is probably best defined as "staying true," or "being alert or sharp." It has the idea of not being distracted, of staying focused on the important goals and objectives.

Once again, read the helpful words of Simon Kistemaker in his *New Testament Commentary*:

> The New Testament concept [to contend] is familiar to his readers. In brief, it means to exert oneself without distraction to attain a goal. It means self-denial to overcome obstacles, to avoid perils, and if need be, to accept martyrdom. Jude implies that the members of the Church must exert themselves in spreading the gospel and defeating heresy.[4]

Contending has within it the idea of intense effort much like one would exert in a wrestling match. Make no mistake: It's a very strong term. Unfortunately, it has come to be used in a negative way when in actuality *contending* for the faith originally meant the idea of being able to clearly *articulate* the faith. Yet remember, there is never to be found a biblical injunction to be *combative* with someone in the family of God.

As a young boy, I can remember how frequently I would fight with my older brother. We didn't just share unkind words . . . we'd really get involved in some knock-down-drag-out fistfights. Blood was not uncommon. I think back on those incidents with sincere and deep regret. How stupid we were, wasting potentially great times together as siblings! There is nothing to be gained by family fighting. Nothing.

Are we wasting time fighting those who are our brothers? This is a delicate issue. We do not want to fight, to cause dissension. Yet we are not to turn the other way when heresy rears its ugly head. We are to stay focused, contending for the faith. In Jude's letter he addressed this need for focus when he wrote, "But you, dear friends, build yourselves up in your most holy faith" (Jude 20).

See what he is saying? The way to fight off heresy is to be clearly focused on the truth. Doctrine builds you up. It puts you in a much better position to relate together.

To contend also carries with it the responsibility of discerning the truth one will contend for and defend. The word *discern* is defined in Funk and Wagnall's dictionary as "to discriminate mentally; to recognize as separate and different." In essence, it is the ability to determine truth from error. It is what Paul meant when he told the believers in Thessalonica, "Test everything. Hold on to the good. Avoid every kind of evil" (1 Thess. 5:21–22).

"Wait a minute!" I can hear someone object. "Jesus told us, 'Do not judge, or you too will be judged.'" But spiritual discernment is a far cry from the harsh, condemnatory, and judgmental attitude Jesus was speaking about in Matthew 7:1–5.

Spiritual discernment is what we read about in Acts 17. Here's what took place: Paul, Silas, and young Timothy had been traveling from city to city preaching and teaching the gospel. They had been stopped by the Holy Spirit from entering the province of Asia and went over to the city of Philippi, where they caused quite a stir and ended up in prison. From there they went to Thessalonica, where their preaching of the truth of the resurrection of Jesus caused a mob scene, and they had to flee in the night. They had arrived in Berea and went straight to the local synagogue to preach

Christ. Luke, the writer of the book of Acts, made a keen observation about the situation:

> Now the Bereans were of more noble character than the Thessalonians, for they received the message with greater eagerness and examined the Scriptures every day to see if what Paul said was true. (Acts 17:11)

Can you imagine the audacity of these Bereans to "examine" what the apostle Paul was teaching to see whether or not it was true! What a judgmental attitude they must have had! How arrogant for them to think they were superior to the apostle Paul and his team!

No . . . not at all. What they exhibited was spiritual discernment. Their seeking to distinguish truth from error and to hold fast to that which is true is commendable. It's the same thing Paul told Titus: "to hold firmly to the trustworthy message as it has been taught, so that he [an elder] can encourage others by sound doctrine and refute those who oppose it" (Titus 1:9).

So I *am* concerned about sound doctrine. I *am* concerned about careful study of the Scriptures. Every Christian should be seeking to obey 2 Timothy 2:15, which says:

> Do your best to present yourself to God as one approved, a workman who does not need to be ashamed and who correctly handles the word of truth.

The key is to be rooted in the foundational doctrines of our faith. Sometimes we can be so concerned with the patching of the stained-glass windows that we overlook the crumbling foundation. Even though the windows are breathtakingly beautiful and that's what the people see, in terms of the longevity of the building the condition of the foundation is far more crucial than the condition of the windows.

The Foundation

At the core of a Christian's belief system are five doctrines:

The Bible

God

Jesus Christ

The Holy Spirit

The redemption of man

These are the issues that are germane to the faith of which Jude wrote. These are truths that must be believed and applied. It is when we rally around these issues that we can most effectively reach the world before us. So this is more than a book on Bible doctrine. It is a book to call men to action.

Think about each of these issues:

The Bible: By believing God has revealed Himself to me, I can base my life on revealed truth.

God: By believing that God exists and that I am created by Him and unto Him, I can, therefore, relate to Him.

Jesus Christ: By believing that Jesus is God and that His life and death provide something for me, I can be in relationship with Him. His characteristics can characterize my life. I can be strong, I can be compassionate, and I can have many other traits modeled after Christ.

The Holy Spirit: God does not make demands of me without providing the means and resources to accomplish these demands. He has given the Holy Spirit to enable us. Therefore I am not an orphan or deserted.

The redemption of man: By understanding my own sinfulness and my need for a redeemer, I can be fully accepted based on the work of Christ on the cross. Through His work I can find both security and significance.

These are the issues of importance. What we believe is far more important than what we are called.

What's in a Name?

If we could become more concerned with issues of the heart than what a man calls himself, what a difference it would make in the body of Christ! We are so caught up in labels and names. And regrettably, once we label we begin to assume things about people based on that label. "Oh, you're a Baptist. I assume you believe such and such." "Ah-ha, so you are a Pentecostal. Surely you believe so and so."

One explanation for why we label each other is that it often keeps us out of involvement in relationships. If I can ascertain that this man is of a certain label, than I can safely justify in my mind why I want nothing to do with him. "He's an Episcopal-metho-bapterian-matic-costal!" we exclaim. "I would be compromising my position *by having anything to do with him!*"

What is particularly saddening is that labels are a form of outward appearance, and they can be very deceiving. A number of years ago I took my family to visit Universal Studios in Hollywood, California. We bought our tickets and scurried through the lines with a childlike excitement. It didn't take long, however, for that excitement to wane.

Out in the back lot, for example, we would see streets and neighborhoods we immediately recognized from some of our favorite TV sit-coms. But to our amazement, once you walked through the front door of these homes, there was nothing but dirt on the other side. The "houses" were nothing more than fronts, facades, fakes. Where we expected to see a living room or a kitchen or a den, we saw wide-open spaces.

We live in a world very much like Universal Studios. As one man put it, "We live in a day in which image rates higher than character and style counts more than real accomplishment. We are impressed with outward appearances and easily distracted from the unspectacular disciplines that lead to excellence. Life is skimmed from the surface, and the depths remain usually unexplored." What we need is a desire to become the kind of men who are willing to go beneath the surface.

Young David in the Old Testament was a man like that. The Bible tells us he was a man after God's own heart. In 1 Samuel the prophet Samuel was appointed by God to anoint the next king. As he went to meet with Jesse, David's father began to bring forth his sons, beginning with the oldest, Eliab. When Eliab stepped forward, Samuel's immediate impression was, *This certainly must be the one God wants. He looks right, he talks right, he smells right, his name even sounds kingly. He has the right air about him. Surely this must be the Lord's anointed.*

What was taking place was the exact same thing that happened when the people of Israel cried to have Saul appointed as king. They had, as

Samuel did in Jesse's tent, a "Universal Studios experience." They were content to look at the appearance, the stature, the demeanor—all of those things a good public relations firm can put in place. But they didn't look to the issue of the heart. After all of the sons except David had passed before Samuel, the prophet asked if there was yet another son.

Jesse remarked that there was one more son, but he was the youngest boy, David. He was not only the youngest in terms of age, but Jesse's answer also implied that he was the despised one, the one who was not capable of any more responsibility than what he had tending the sheep out on the hillside. But Samuel demanded that David be brought before him, and sure enough, David was the one God chose.

Why did God choose him? I can think of at least three reasons. First, David was a man who was spiritually mature. That didn't mean he walked around with drab clothing and a long face, speaking in pious tones. Rather, he was a "man after God's own heart." I take that to mean that his heart beat with God's heart. What grieved God grieved David. When God said to David, "I want you to change something," or "I want you to go somewhere," there was never an argument or debate. David was a man who moved with the will of God. When you're a man after God's own heart, His desires are your desires. God doesn't need to keep dealing with you on an issue. A spiritually mature man is not one who never sins but one who readily repents and seeks the Lord's enabling and empowering to not continue in that sin any longer.

Later, when the prophet Nathan confronted David concerning his sin with Bathsheba, David repented and confessed his sin and sought the Lord's mercy. When King Saul was confronted concerning his sin and disobedience to the Lord, he became fearful and fretful, but he did not repent. That is the difference between spiritual maturity and immaturity.

Not only was David spiritually mature, he was also a man of true humility. He was willing to continue to serve where God placed him. In 1 Samuel 16:19, we are told that after David had been annointed the next king of Israel he simply returned to shepherd the sheep. The psalmist tells us in Psalm 78:70–71 that God took him from shepherding the sheep to being the shepherd of His people, Israel. That shows us that David wasn't about to elevate himself; instead he waited for the Lord to move him into that area of responsibility. God calls us to be faithful with the little things and to trust Him, remembering that before God will ever give me a scepter, I must be faithful with a staff.

The third characteristic of David was that he was a man of integrity. Psalm 78:72 tells us: "And David shepherded them with integrity of heart; with skillful hands he led them."

This verse paints for us a picture of sincerity and of moral completeness. It communicates that you are responsible on the hillside even when no one else is around. It is the ability to be alone with responsibility and hold it in an honest and careful way.

Why this treatise on David? To underscore the importance of *what's inside.* David was a lowly shepherd boy. Believe me, there was nothing special about that name, nothing impressive about that label. On the contrary, to label him would have caused people to miss out on one of God's most amazing servants. In today's world, I wonder who we have labeled in such a way to limit his effectiveness for their Lord. I wonder who could be building into our lives through relationship if it weren't for the branding we've given him.

Are we concerned with what a man calls himself (or what others call him), or with what a man believes?

Conclusion

These chapters have attempted to set the stage for the heart of this book, the five chapters that follow on the five foundational doctrines of the faith. What you will read are the facts of the faith. And it is these facts that affect all of us who believe them. Our faith is based on fact, but it is meant to be experienced and acted upon.

This is the faith that changes men's lives. This is the faith that moved my family and me from the secure setting of a pastorate in New Jersey to the relatively unsettled environment of a new church home in Colorado. The congregation in New Jersey *loved* us. From a mere human perspective, it was very difficult to move on.

The church in Colorado had a long, rich history with many challenges. This was not the peaceful, serene setting we had just left back on the East Coast. My daughter, only a little girl at the time, said to me, "Daddy, I know this move was the right thing. I know this is what God wants." She paused. "So why does it hurt, Daddy?" Sometimes God's heavenly plans do not make any earthly sense.

This is where faith is tested. It is a situation where intellect and emotion don't line up. Yet through it all, there is a settled sense that "This is what God wants me to do; this is where He wants me to be." Even though it hurts and may even seem senseless, you know that it is God's wisdom that dictates the right or wrong of the decision.

It is this faith that will cause a man to walk away from his six-figure income to earn minimum wage working in the inner city. It is this faith that will cause a guy to refuse a deal because it is shady at best. It is this faith that is anchored in the eternal, that gives more value to incorruptible treasures than to the corruptible ones of this world. It is faith that will cause a man to keep plugging away . . . to stay the course.

It is this faith, the rock-solid foundation, that will keep the whole building strong and secure . . .

Even the stained-glass windows.

Personal Evaluation

Sometimes schoolteachers give what they call a "pretest." This is where you are tested on material before it is actually taught, just to see how much you know about a given subject beforehand. Let's take a little pretest on what we are about to learn in the second part of this book. Just to be sure you're not at a complete loss, I have included some "hints" with each question (I'll bet you never had a schoolteacher that nice!).

1. Write down two or three key statements concerning what you believe about the Bible. *(Hint: Maybe the following terms will be helpful—Word of God, inerrant, inspired, revelation.)*

   a. _____

   _____

   _____

   b. _____

   _____

THE AWESOME POWER OF SHARED BELIEFS

c. _____

_____

2. Write down what you believe about God. (*Hint: Think about the following words—Trinity, Creator, immortal, omnipotent, omnipresent, immutable, eternal, loving, just.*)

a. _____

_____

b. _____

c. _____

_____

3. Write down what you believe about Jesus Christ. (*Hint: Key concepts might be virgin birth, fully God, fully man, why He came, His miracles, His teachings, His death and resurrection.*)

a. _____

_____

b. _____

_____

c. _____

_____

4. What are your beliefs concerning the Holy Spirit? (*Hint: Godhead, indwelling, filling.*)

a. _____

_____

b. _____

_____

c. _____

_____

5. How would you sum up your beliefs concerning man and his need for salvation? (*Hint: sin, the Fall of man, redemption, eternal life.*)

a. _____

_____

b. _____
_____
c. _____
_____

In the Group

1. Have you ever had any experiences where a faulty foundation led to countless headaches? Share some of your more memorable experiences with the group. This sharing could have the potential of being very sad or quite hilarious.

2. When Jude said we should "contend for the faith," what do you think he meant by "the faith"? Be as specific as possible. Try to use practical terms in your definition. How much or how little is held in that description? In your experience, do people tend to add to the meaning of the faith, take away from it, or pretty much leave it as it is?

3. What were your impressions of the Apostles' Creed? How about the Nicene Creed? Prior to this reading, had you had much exposure to either of these documents? Share your experience with these two creeds. Are they good documents or not? Are they helpful or damaging? Do you see them used much today? Why or why not?

4. How would you define the word *contend*? Tell the group a good, one-word synonym for that word and then tell them two or three things that contend does *not* mean. Have you ever seen this verse being misunderstood and causing dissension among the ranks of Christians? Share your experience with the group. How could the dissension have been avoided? What did you learn from the incident?

5. We listed five essential doctrines as the foundation of the Christian faith: the Bible, God, Jesus Christ, the Holy Spirit, and the redemption of man. Do you agree with that list, or would you

add one or two more or subtract any that you believe are less important?

6. Divide up into groups of two or three and pray for one another. This time, I have a very specific request for both of you: Be sure to pray for maximum understanding of the next five chapters. They are the heart and soul of the whole book, so I hope you'll find them as helpful as possible in communicating the truth. Check up on each other's prayer requests as well. I hope this is becoming a very special time for you and your partner.

Memory Verse: "Dear friends, although I was very eager to write to you about the salvation we share, I felt I had to write and urge you to contend for the faith that was once entrusted to the saints" (Jude 3).

Part Two

The Basis of Unity

The Bible*

by Dr. Bruce L. Shelley

IN A.D. 303, when it was illegal to be a Christian, the Roman emperor Diocletian issued a decree that he hoped would extinguish the spreading flames of Christianity. The primary objective was the seizure and destruction of the Christian Scriptures.

Later that year, officials enforced the decree in North Africa. One of the targets was a man named Felix, bishop of Tibjuca, a village near Carthage. The mayor of the town ordered Felix to hand over his Scriptures. Though some judges were willing to accept scraps of parchment, Felix refused to surrender even that much of the Word of God at the insistence of mere men.

The Roman authorities finally shipped Felix to Italy, where he paid for his stubbornness with his life. On August 30, as the record puts it, "with pious obstinacy" he laid down his life rather than surrender his Gospels.[1]

In our day when the Bible is so readily available, we may find Felix's dogged determination mystifying. It does highlight, however, a fact of central importance for a proper understanding of the Christian faith: Christianity is inextricably linked to the Bible.

---

* This chapter is adapted from Chapters 2 and 3 of *Theology for Ordinary People* by Dr. Bruce L. Shelley, © 1993 Bruce L. Shelley. Used by permission of InterVarsity Press, P.O. Box 1400, Downers Grove, Illinois 60515.

The Bible isn't the only way God has revealed Himself, however. He has also given us His general revelation, which we find in His creation. The natural order—the world of sights and smells and sounds—is filled with hints and clues of the presence and power of God: the lightning flash, the spider's web, the galaxy's order. These and countless other impressions from the universe are whispers of the God who made them all. The ancient Hebrews sang of this wonder: "The heavens declare the glory of God; the skies proclaim the work of his hands" (Ps. 19:1).

Paul, the early Christian evangelist, agreed. Since the creation of the world, he said, "God's invisible qualities—his eternal power and divine nature—have been clearly seen" (Rom. 1:20). People detect these qualities in the things He has made.

The tribespeople of Ecuador and Indonesia, then, are not entirely misled in fearing the spirits of the forests and streams. The visible world does veil an invisible one. Their sin, like our own, lies in worshiping and serving created things rather than the Creator. The brush strokes of nature are designed to introduce us to the Artist. He set us in the world of wonders, not to make us idolaters, but to make us thankful.

Of all the things God has made, nothing carries His image quite like human creatures. The power of reason, by which we question God's existence, is itself a sign of God's handiwork. Reason alone is ill-equipped to sit in judgment of God's truth, however. No human mind is capable of that. But our ability to think at all is a reflection of God's character. He is no irrational force but the source of all reason. If that were not so, we could never understand His self-disclosure.

Without reason, we have no basis for insisting that one faith is any better or worse than another. All talk of God or religion would be so much meaningless babbling. But if God is rational, we can expect His message to us to be reasonable.

In the end, then, general revelation from God points us to His existence and character but it can only take us so far. To know Him better—what He's like, how to relate to Him, and what He expects of us—We need a more specific and authoritative revelation. And that's where the Bible comes in.

The Authority of the Bible

The Christian faith holds that God has chosen to speak to human beings not only through creation, but also through a special stream of human history recorded in the Bible. We call this "special" revelation because it carries a special message from God to the ancient people of Israel and to all people ever since its writing.

In other words, the God who inhabits eternity has Himself bridged the chasm into time. He decided to communicate with men and women in a way they can understand—through human history. One special segment of human experience became His channel of communication and reached a climax in His ultimate message: "The Word became flesh and made his dwelling among us" (John 1:14)—perhaps the most astonishing statement in the whole Bible.

When the Bible uses the expression "the Word of God," it means what Christians call "God's revelation," the words or actions of God through which He makes Himself known to men and women. We read that by His Word God created the heavens and the earth. "By the word of the LORD were the heavens made, their starry host by the breath of his mouth" (Ps. 33:6). God also spoke to the Hebrew prophets, whose constant claim was "the Word of the Lord came to me." Finally, in "the last days" He spoke through Jesus Christ, His special Son (see Heb. 1:1–2). By announcing this revelation from God, Christians make spiritual life available to those who believe the message. People find genuine faith in the way they "hear" the Word and gain new life by its power (see Rom. 10:17).

The Word has the unique ability to bring people face to face with the living God and to hold them accountable for their lives before Him. We call this power to demand human obedience "divine authority." In ordinary life, we settle disputes by appealing to an authority. It may be a book of law, a medical journal, or a flight schedule. In any case, an authority possesses the power to settle an issue. So in matters about God and His relationship with men and women, the authority is the Word of God.

Christians have always believed that the Scriptures are more than a mere record of the Word of God. They *are* the Word of God in the sense that they convey the message of God's acts, and that they act on the souls of people, calling for a response to God. It's not possible for scholars to extract somehow the great truths from the history of Israel or from Jesus' teaching in order to create general religious principles for humanity and then discard the biblical events as so many myths. Truth is in the biblical story, and power is in its telling. That's why the Bible sets the standard for beliefs in Christianity.

Obviously, people can read the Bible simply as ancient literature. They do it all the time. But when Christians speak of the Bible as the Word of God, they are talking about what C. S. Lewis once called "getting the focus right." It is possible, he said, for a person to contend that a poem is nothing but black marks on white paper. And such an argument might be convincing before an audience that couldn't read. You could examine the print under a microscope or analyze the paper and ink, but this sort of analysis would never reveal anything you could call "a poem." Those who can read, however, will continue to insist that poems exist.[2]

One of the terms Christians use to describe this special focus of the Bible is *inspiration.* By that they mean that the Bible came to the writers as a result of God's initiative, not because of any human plan. The Bible itself often says that about the writings of the prophets and apostles. Second Timothy 3:16, for example, says Scripture was "God-breathed," which means it was produced by the power or energy of the almighty God.

Another passage, 2 Peter 1:20–21, uses a different image for God's activity. It says the prophets were "carried along" by God's Spirit like a ship propelled by winds filling its sails. Inspiration, then, stands for all the activities of God in selecting, moving, and imparting His Word to the prophets of the Old Testament and the apostles of the New Testament in the course of their writing the Scriptures.

This activity of God seldom overwhelmed the authors. They were not carried away into a mystical world of heavenly truths. They retained their own individuality, with styles and perspectives uniquely their own. Some were scholars; others were peasants. Some were rural, others were urban. Each brought personal vocabulary, temperament, and experience to the special work of communicating the Word.

As a consequence, Christians hold that the Bible is both a divine and a human book. It communicates the Word of God, yet it calls for study like any other piece of literature. It is both the Word of God and the words of human beings. It demands submission and faith, but at the same time it requires study and interpretation.

The Bible often speaks of the spiritual realities of the "hidden world." To make these realms intelligible to us, it employs symbolic or metaphorical language. And that poses a problem for many people. If we take these expressions literally, they will mislead us. We use no scales to measure the weight of an argument and no mathematics to calculate the height of a lofty ideal. We never get a suntan from the glow of a sunny disposition or the illumination of a brilliant scholar. In day-to-day conversation, we seem to manage metaphors quite well. Why should we have so much trouble understanding the Bible?

Some people, when they recognize biblical metaphor, tend to dilute the image to some vapid moralism. They have the good sense to realize that "hellfire" is a metaphor, but they unwisely conclude that it means nothing more serious than inward remorse, something we often experience this side of the grave. Or they rightly think that Paul spoke metaphorically when he said Christians are "raised" to "walk in newness of life." But they misunderstand him completely if they think he meant the Christian faith consists of nothing more than a respectable life in acceptable society.

This type of interpretation is so common that it creates a distinct impression that some people don't have trouble with biblical metaphors so much as with biblical miracles. And if that's true, these people will never understand the Bible or Christianity. For example, if you subtract the miraculous elements from Hindu pantheism, all the essential beliefs remain. The same is obviously true in the case of humanism, since by its very definition it leaves no room for miracles. But a Christianity without miracles is not Christianity.

The Big Picture

At first glance, the Bible is a strange sort of book. It contains sixty-six smaller books written by approximately forty authors over a period of sixteen hundred years. The first thirty-nine books, called the Old Testament, were originally Jewish Scriptures and were written mostly in Hebrew. The twenty-seven books called the New Testament were written later by Christians in Greek.

The Old Testament is often divided into the Law (the first five books), the Prophets, and the Writings, which include the popular Psalms and Proverbs. The New Testament can be divided into the Gospels (four of them) and the Epistles (or letters). The Acts of the Apostles serves as a historical bridge from the Gospels to the Epistles, and the last book, Revelation, provides a unique climax to the whole collection.

The thread running through the sixty-six books is the story of human rebellion against God and God's merciful acts intended to elicit repentance and faith in men and women. The story is no myth. It really happened. That is one reason we say Christianity is a historical religion. God's message about Himself and His reconciliation of rebellious human beings is an unfolding history of a nation called Israel and a person called Jesus. *The Christian faith cannot be divorced from this biblical story.*

Biblical history is unlike our modern view of history in that a modern historian is supposed to give an objective account of the facts of his or her period. But biblical history is *interpreted history.* Biblical authors have a point of view; they share a testimony as well as a story.

The authors were selective, therefore, in their choice of material. Rather than focus on movements of the mighty ancient empires—Assyria, Babylon, Persia, Egypt, Greece, and Rome—they mentioned them only as they impinged on the relatively inconsequential (from a human perspective) Israelite communities in Palestine. The Bible isn't concerned with the wisdom, wealth, or might of this world but with the salvation provided by God.

The Start of the Story

The story begins with time itself: "In the beginning God created the heavens and the earth." And on the sixth day of creation, the Lord God crowned His work by fashioning men and women in His own image. When God checked on His handiwork, He saw that it was very good—but not for long. Only three chapters into the story, human beings stumble into moral ruin. The rest of the Bible is about the rescue of the rebels.

After the initial sin of the original pair, Adam and Eve, their children plunged into the grossest immorality. God even came to regret that He had made the human pair, so He decided to destroy the earth with a flood. With an eye on the future, however, He arranged for the survival of a single household—Noah and his immediate family.

Even this dreadful judgment failed to cure men and women of their depravity. Noah's descendants took the same path as Adam and Eve. In their pride, they refused to accept the Lord as God and worship Him.

As a result, somewhere around 2000 B.C., God implemented a new strategy in His dealings with men and women. He turned to a specific people who became His new beachhead in the world.

That nation began with a single man, Abraham. While living in Ur of the Chaldees (ancient Mesopotamia and modern Iraq), Abraham heard God's call: "Leave your country, your people, and your father's household and go to the land I will show you." Then God offered Abraham a promise. "I will make you into a great nation and I will bless you. . . . I will bless those who bless you, and whoever curses you I will curse; and all peoples on earth will be blessed through you" (Gen. 12:1–3). The remainder of the Bible is the unfolding of this promise, called the *covenant.*

Abraham passed on this promise to his son Isaac, born to Abraham and Sarah when they were beyond childbearing years. Then Isaac repeated the promise to his son Jacob, whose name was also Israel. Finally, Jacob passed the promise to his twelve sons, the heads of the twelve tribes of Israel.

Through the treachery of his brothers, Joseph, one of Israel's sons, was sold into slavery in Egypt. But, as Joseph himself put it, what his brothers intended for evil, God intended for good. Joseph the slave became Joseph the vice pharaoh of Egypt.

Joseph probably came into power during the reign of the Hyksos rulers (about 1700 B.C.), the foreign "shepherd kings" who ruled between Egyptian dynasties. These favorable years ended, however, when "a new king, who did not know about Joseph," came to power in Egypt (Exod. 1:8). This new pharaoh, perhaps Rameses II, conscripted the Hebrews into labor camps and stone quarries. And the people of Israel cried out to God for deliverance.

The deliverance came from an unexpected source, Pharaoh's own palace. After training in the royal courts and enduring lonely years in the Sinai wilderness, Moses was ready to fulfill his destiny. He heard the call from the Lord and delivered God's message to Pharaoh: "Let my people go!" Pharaoh's determined resistance provoked God to send a series of plagues, the last one killing all the firstborn sons in Egypt except those of the Hebrews. Jews still celebrate this event in the Passover holiday. Pharaoh's resistance finally crumbled. He let the people go.

The Israelites were hardly on the road, however, when Pharaoh reverted to his former stubbornness and pursued the bedraggled band of ex-slaves. With the sea before them and the Egyptian troops closing in from behind, the Israelites watched as Moses stretched out his staff and the sea parted for them and then crashed down on the pursuing army.

The Covenant at Sinai

The ragged multitude of grumbling Israelites eventually reached the foot of Mount Sinai, where Moses had met the Lord at the burning bush years before. Here God gave Israel three special gifts: the renewed covenant, a moral law, and an atoning sacrifice.

The covenant came first. "You have seen what I did to the Egyptians," God told Israel, "and how I bore you up on eagles' wings and brought you to myself. Now, therefore, if you obey my voice and keep my covenant, you shall be my own possession among all peoples" (Exod. 19:4–5 RSV). The people happily accepted God's covenant.

Keeping this covenant meant obeying God's moral law. Its essence was the Ten Commandments, which gave Israel the essentials for maintaining a right relationship with God and with people.

But what if the Israelites broke the moral law? That was the purpose of the sacrificial system and the ceremonial law. Every dramatic action of the system carried some message and looked forward to that final, once-for-all sacrifice of the Perfect Lamb that God would one day offer.

With the law in hand, the chosen people headed for their promised land. When they reached the border of Palestine, however, they halted in faithless fear. The inhabitants of the land seemed like giants to them. The Israelites' unbelief provoked the Lord. He condemned His people to wander in the wilderness until every adult of that generation perished. Only after forty years, under the leadership of Joshua, did the *people* of promise enter the *land* of promise.

The first order of business for Joshua was a conquest of the local inhabitants, the Canaanites. After a series of brilliant military victories, Joshua parceled out land to the twelve tribes of Israel. But he failed to subdue the local populations. As a result, the Canaanites persisted as a constant source of political and religious irritation.

The book of Judges illustrates this repeatedly. Time and again the Israelites succumbed to the worship of Baal and Ashtaroth, the local Canaanite fertility gods. The Lord would respond by allowing an oppressor to gain the upper hand over one of the tribes. When the people called on the Lord for deliverance, He would send a judge, a military leader, to break the bonds of the oppressor.

After two hundred years of such ups and downs, and especially their defeat at the hands of the Philistines, the Israelites had had enough. They cried out for a king, "that we also may be like all the nations" (1 Sam. 8:20 RSV).

The Age of Kings (1050–586 B.C.)

God complied with Israel's request and gave them a king. Saul was the strongest, handsomest man in the land. Though he was somewhat successful in his military exploits, he was not always content to obey the Lord. Three times he specifically disregarded direct commands of God. His downfall began when a young shepherd boy named David won the praise of Israel by defeating the Philistine hero Goliath. Wild with jealousy, Saul spent his last years as king haplessly hounding David, the anointed heir to his throne. It was not a pretty picture.

Under David's dynamic leadership, Israel subdued its enemies and extended its borders from the "river of Egypt" (Egypt's frontier *wadi* extending into the Sinai) to the River Euphrates in Mesopotamia.

David was more than an ancient warlord. He was also an artist— a musician and poet. He had a sensitive spirit, and he was generous with his enemies and loyal to his friends. Above all, he was devoted to the Lord. Aside from his tragic sin against Bathsheba and Uriah, his life was marked by exceptional godliness. The psalms he wrote reveal an unsurpassed depth of spirituality.

God made a special promise to David: "Your house and your kingdom shall be made sure for ever before me" (2 Sam. 7:16 RSV). This became the keynote of Israel's hope for the next four hundred years. God would sustain the Davidic line until the ultimate triumph of the Messiah, the special leader in Israel's future.

David was succeeded by his son Solomon. Gifted with unusual wisdom, Solomon brought Israel to a zenith of economic prosperity, peace, and strength. Unfortunately, he achieved much of his success by conscripted labor. Solomon's major weakness, however, was women. In defiance of the Lord's prohibition of intermarriage, he kept a harem of foreign princesses, and they "turned his heart after other gods" (1 Kings 11:4).

Rehoboam, Solomon's son, inherited his father's troubles as well as his throne. People from the north of Israel, who had groaned under Solomon's oppressive measures, demanded a reprieve from Rehoboam. The king replied with threats of a heavier yoke for the necks of such grumblers. He succeeded in provoking the northern ten tribes into seceding from the Davidic dynasty. Only 120 years after its beginning, the kingdom of Israel was irreparably split. Only the tribes of Judah and Benjamin remained loyal to the throne established by God's covenant.

A former government official named Jeroboam assumed the leadership of the northern kingdom, sometimes called Israel, sometimes called Ephraim. He faced problems immediately. The temple Solomon had built was in Jerusalem, Rehoboam's capital. If Jeroboam's subjects made pilgrimages there, he feared he would lose their loyalty. So he built two alternative sanctuaries in which he installed altars resting on golden calves: one in Dan and the other in Bethel.

This relieved his political problem but ensured his infamy in the annals of Israel's history. The author of the books of 1 and 2 Kings makes this crystal clear. Without any exception, the kings of the north "did evil in the eyes of the LORD." Often the author gets specific by charging some king with "walking in the ways of [Jeroboam] and in his sin, which he had caused Israel to commit" (1 Kings 15:26).

The Lord finally sent judgment on Israel in the form of the powerful Assyrians. In 722 B.C., Shalmaneser V besieged and destroyed Samaria and deported twenty-seven thousand inhabitants of the nation (see 2 Kings 17:3–6). The ten tribes were assimilated into native populations.

The southern kingdom, Judah, was a different story, at least in part. Though the dynasty of David continued, his descendants did not inherit his devotion. The authors of Kings and Chronicles tell us that most "did evil in the eyes of the LORD" by tolerating idolatry. Despite efforts of occasional reformers such as Hezekiah and Josiah, Judah also provoked the Lord. Judgment came in the form of the mighty ruler Nebuchadnezzar, king of Babylon, who razed Jerusalem in 586 B.C.

What happened to God's promise to David that his throne would never end? Had God abandoned His people and His promise? During these years of crisis, prophets appeared in Judah offering an answer to that question. Isaiah, for example, preached that all nations—even the mighty Assyrian empire—were merely tools of God's plan for the final salvation of humankind. He said Judah's suffering would produce "a remnant of Israel" that would return to their homeland and preside over a coming age of righteousness and peace.

Though the northern kingdom was entirely lost, Judah suffered exile for only seventy years. When Cyrus of Persia conquered Babylon, he allowed the Jews to return and rebuild their city and temple. This they did under the leadership of Zerubbabel (who rebuilt the temple), Ezra (who brought the people back to the Law), and Nehemiah (who rebuilt the walls of Jerusalem). Here, under the prophetic ministries of Haggai, Zechariah, and Malachi, the Old Testament comes to a conclusion.

Intertestamental Times

Though most Bibles simply add the New Testament to the prophecies of the Old, nearly four hundred years of history unfolded between Malachi and Matthew. We may view this period as God's preparation of the world for the coming of the Messiah, Jesus of Nazareth.

At the end of the Old Testament, Judah was a tiny vassal state of the mighty Persian empire. So it remained until 333 B.C., when Alexander the Great of Macedonia (northern Greece) subdued Persia and assumed authority over the Jews. Upon Alexander's death, his power passed on to four of his generals. The Jews, heirs of ancient Israel, fell under the jurisdiction of Ptolemy, whose state centered in Alexandria, Egypt.

In a sense, Alexander's conquests prepared the world for the Christian faith. First, Greek philosophy spread into conquered lands, and Greek ideas of monotheism, immortality, and morality formed a point of contact between Christianity and the pagan world.

Second, Greek reigned as the common trade language in all the Mediterranean world and remained so for nearly five hundred years. This enabled people like the apostle Paul to preach in a single language over a broad geographical area. During the Ptolemaic period, scholars translated the Old Testament into Greek (the Septuagint) and thus made the Bible available to hosts of new readers.

In 198 B.C. the Seleucids, the Syrian segment of Alexander's empire, annexed Palestine. Within a generation the Syrian king, Antiochus Epiphanes, instituted a policy of oppression against Jews and outlawed their religion. When soldiers attempted to force Mattathias, the high priest, to sacrifice to pagan gods, he and his family instigated a rebellion. By means of guerrilla warfare, the so-called Maccabean Revolt successfully shed the shackles of the Seleucids and established the free state of Israel.

Freedom, however was short-lived. The Maccabean rulers fell into the same trap as their forefathers. Corruption helped to guarantee their eventual fall, which came in 63 B.C. at the hands of the Romans. Twenty-three years later the Roman Senate passed the scepter to Herod the Great, "king of the Jews," who ruled the land when Jesus was born in Bethlehem.

Jesus of Nazareth

The story of Jesus, His disciples, and the early development of Christianity is recorded in the pages of the New Testament. Two of the Gospels—Matthew and Luke—attribute the birth of Jesus to an act of God. The Lord spoke to a Jewish peasant girl, Mary, and her husband-to-be, Joseph. He told them that by the power of the Holy Spirit she would give birth to a son and they were to name him *Yeshua* (Jesus), which in Hebrew means "the Lord saves." According to the Gospels, these descendants of David did just as they were told. And God miraculously gave them a son.

Beyond these birth narratives of Matthew and Luke, we know almost nothing about Jesus' early years. When He was nearly thirty, however, His cousin John began to preach in the Judean wilderness and baptize in the Jordan River. He told the crowds who went out to hear him speak that he was a herald for a leader still to come.

Jesus' own baptism by John proved to be a profound spiritual experience. Immediately afterward, He suffered satanic assaults for forty days in the wilderness and then launched His three-year mission in Israel. The first year was marked by relative obscurity, the second by popularity, and the third by adversity.

During the first year Jesus concentrated on two objectives: reaching out to numbers of people and gathering a small band of disciples—including Peter, Matthew, and John the son of Zebedee. After a few months in the south, Jesus concentrated on the villages of Galilee in the north, away from the official Judaism centered in its hub, Jerusalem.

As His reputation spread the second year, He gave Himself to wider circles of preaching, teaching, and working miracles. The theme of His message was "the gospel of the kingdom." The true kingdom, He said, is the personal reign of God in human lives; He said He had come to inaugurate that rule. The arrival of the kingdom was the fulfillment of the Old Testament hope. But in order to "receive," "enter," or "inherit" the kingdom, men and women had to repent and believe, humbly accepting its privileges and submitting to its demands like little children.

In teaching His disciples, Jesus explained what it meant to live as people of the kingdom. Perhaps the best example of the new law of the kingdom appears in His Sermon on the Mount, found in Matthew's Gospel. A disciple's righteousness, He said, is unlike the religions of the Pharisees and the pagans. The Jewish leaders called Pharisees practiced a strict faith that often slipped into hypocrisy. In sharp contrast, pagans, who lived without the guidance of the Law, used religion as an excuse for selfish gratification. Righteousness, Jesus told His disciples, must spring from a new heart.

Jesus' miracles were themselves a type of teaching. Most of them were healings used as signs of God's kingdom and Jesus' authority. The impact of these "signs and wonders" carried Jesus to the heights of His popularity when He fed five thousand Passover pilgrims. The people were so elated they tried to make Jesus king. Jesus, however, knew that the people totally misunderstood His mission. He withdrew quietly to more isolated regions in order to inform His close friends about His true purpose.

Jesus' popularity with the people provoked the Jewish authorities to jealousy and led to the last phase of His public ministry: adversity. Herod Antipas, the ruler of Galilee, feared that Jesus might be the Messiah whom John the Baptist had predicted. So, with the help of some of the Pharisees, he laid plans to arrest Jesus and kill Him. Jesus learned of the plot, however, and fled to Judea with His disciples.

After several months of preaching, Jesus made His final pilgrimage to Jerusalem for Passover. Accompanied by a large procession, He entered the temple, where He drove out the peddlers of sacrificial animals. On the eve of Passover, Jesus and His twelve disciples celebrated their last meal together. Late that night, soldiers sent by the high priest arrested Jesus.

Before the Sanhedrin, the Jewish high court, Jesus was convicted of blasphemy. Since the Sanhedrin had no authority to execute Him, they rushed Him to the Roman governor, Pontius Pilate, who sentenced Him to death by crucifixion. Soldiers carried out that order: a painful death on a cross.

The Birth of Christianity

Within days, rumors were circulating in Jerusalem that Jesus was no longer dead; He had risen from the grave. The rumors were absolutely correct. The disciples had regathered, and two months later, empowered by the Holy Spirit, they began preaching in Jerusalem's synagogues that Jesus was the promised Messiah; God had confirmed it by raising Him from the dead. Forgiveness of sins and the power of the Spirit, they said, were available to anyone who repented and accepted Jesus as Lord.

Among the new believers were some who spoke Greek. They were called Hellenists. Their increasing numbers alarmed the Jewish authorities. One Hellenist leader named Stephen was stoned to death by an angry mob after he dared to challenge Jewish traditions. The instigator of this assault was a Pharisee, Saul of Tarsus. Intent on destroying this new "heresy," Saul (called Paul after his conversion) set out for Damascus to arrest the Christians there. But on the way, he had a vivid encounter with the resurrected Jesus—an encounter that transformed him into a zealous Christian.

Through Paul's tireless missionary efforts, Christianity spread from its Jewish roots in Judea into Gentile cities, from Antioch in Syria to Rome, the imperial capital. When he was unable to visit the fledgling churches, Paul wrote letters to encourage or instruct them. In most cities, he faced persecution from pagans or from his fellow Jews. Upon his return from a third missionary journey, Jewish leaders secured his imprisonment in Jerusalem. From there Roman authorities moved him to Caesarea, a coastal town, and later to Rome to await trial. He died during Nero's persecution of Christians but left his mark upon Christianity through the theology strikingly expressed in his letters.

This is the story that ties together the sixty-six books of the Bible and discloses the great truths of the Christian faith.

Conclusion

Out of the depths of his agony, Job, an ancient Near Eastern patriarch, sobbed and spoke:

> If only I knew where to find him;
>   if only I could go to his dwelling!
> I would state my case before him
>   and fill my mouth with arguments.
> I would find out what he would answer me,
>   and consider what he would say.
>   Job 23:3–5

This ancient tragedy, the story of Job's losses of property and health and family, is a striking reminder of the fact that our human horizons are too narrow to provide a satisfying view of life and its sorrows. Job's discovery that human wisdom alone offers no adequate explanation of life's meaning is profoundly Christian.

In one sense, men and women are never prepared to hear from the spiritual world until they have discovered secularism's silence. Yet they share a universal concern: *How can I contact reality? Where can I find God?*

The world teems with religions attempting to answer these questions. Christians believe the Creator of heaven and earth has not left humanity to die in what Bertrand Russell would call "cosmic silence." God has spoken to us. He has chosen to disclose Himself to men and women. Job's question, then, is not the appropriate one to ask. The real question is not "How can we find God?" but rather, "How has God revealed Himself to us?"

We have seen that His revelation is twofold. God has communicated to us through the world (general revelation) and through His Word (special revelation).

Job came to see that. At one point in his depression he looked for God in order to state his case. But when he finally encountered the Lord, he learned that in the presence of God, a man does not fill his mouth with words but with wonder.

Personal Evaluation

Answer the following questions as honestly as possible:

1. Do you believe the Bible is God's written Word to us today?

   Yes   No

2. Do you set aside regular time to read the Bible and reflect on what it teaches?

   Never   Seldom   Sometimes   Always

3. Are you satisfied with the amount of time you put into reading your Bible?

   Dissatisfied   Okay   Satisfied

4. Write down the last thing you learned from the Bible by reading it by yourself.

   _____

   _____

   How long ago did you learn this truth?

   A long time ago   Awhile back   Recently

5. Is there something you can do to give higher priority to time with the Word? Jot down a few ideas that will help get you on the right path.

   _____

   _____

   _____

In the Group

1. If your group is one that is somewhat familiar with the Bible, begin by going around the circle and sharing your favorite verse and a brief reason why it is your favorite. If your group is relatively unfamiliar with the Bible, begin by going around the circle and recalling the most significant thought you read in this particular chapter.

2. What is the hardest issue for you to deal with in accepting that the Bible is the Word of God? Be honest with your struggles if you have them in this area. Perhaps someone else in the group can share how he felt the same way and how he came to resolve the specific issue at hand.

3. How would you describe inspiration to someone who is completely unfamiliar with the concept? How does biblical inspiration differ from other uses of the same word?

4. As you read through Dr. Shelley's overview of the Bible, what stands out as your favorite part of the Old Testament story? How about your favorite part of Christ's life, as recorded in the New Testament? How has this impacted your life?

5. Reflect on what you learned in this chapter by sharing with the group any differences that reading it will make in your life. Did this chapter spark you to engage in more personal Bible reading? Are you committing to a Bible-study group in order to learn even more? What difference will this chapter make in your day-to-day life?

6. Conclude your group discussion with a season of prayer. Be sure to check in with your partner, once again exchanging requests and updates.

Memory Verse: "All Scripture is God-breathed and is useful for teaching, rebuking, correcting and training in righteousness, so that the man of God may be thoroughly equipped for every good work" (2 Tim. 3:16–17 NIV).

Chapter**Five**

God*

by Dr. Max Anders

IMAGINE I AM AN ARCHAEOLOGIST and I am tramping through the steaming jungle of Central America. I have flown to Guatemala, gathered my supplies, hired my support team, and begun forging my way inland toward the site of an undiscovered ancient Mayan city.

I am famous for my archaeological exploits. I've written a number of archaeological books . . . several of them textbooks on the modern science of archaeology and several describing the actual discoveries I've made in other locations. I am a Hoosier. My nickname is "Indiana Max."

We 're into our third week, hacking our way through near-impenetrable vegetation. The support team is approaching exhaustion. The heat rises to 110 degrees during the day and cools to only 90 degrees at night. With 100 percent humidity, there's never any relief from the oppression. The plants either stick us, stab us, or slice us. There are snakes above and lizards below. Then there are the insects.

---

* This chapter is excerpted, with permission, from a book written by Dr. Max Anders entitled, *God: Knowing Our Creator,* from the *We Believe: Basics in Christianity* series, published by Thomas Nelson Publishers, © 1995 by Max E. Anders.

Mosquitoes swarm us like banshees coming after the soul of a newly departed sinner. Ants gouge us, and chiggers and ticks lie in wait to have us for dinner. And the noise . . . The constant din of a million crawling creatures begins to pierce our minds like a burglar alarm going off in the middle of our heads.

Three days later, feet burning, eyes stinging, muscles screaming their rebellion, we finally hack our way through a wall of hundred-year-old vines, and on the other side, rising like a great green diamond out of the jungle floor, is a huge pyramid covered with centuries of lush, tropical undergrowth.

I take a compass reading, and we start hacking our way south. Seven hours later, we come to another pyramid. The afternoon of the third day, we find another one, and the fourth day still another, forming the four corners of a huge ceremonial courtyard . . . a great square of ancient Mayan life. Connecting the four corners is a raised sidewalk that meets in the center of the four pyramids at a huge altar made of a single piece of stone. I have found the ceremonial center of an ancient city, lost centuries ago, lying silent and alone, unseen and unknown by modern man.

Here's the big question: How did I know this ancient city was here? Why did I go to such effort? Why did we push ourselves to the breaking point, both physically and mentally, to reach this place? Did I just fly to a random spot on the Central American coast and start hacking my way inland? Not likely. That's a good way to die in the jaws of an unforgiving jungle. No, I was flying over the jungle one day, coming back from another expedition in the neighboring country of Belize. From twenty-five thousand feet up, the jungle floor has a consistent randomness to it. No two square miles are alike, and yet it's all alike. It's different but always the same.

But then, on the horizon ahead, I saw some hills. Four of them. Of course, there are hills throughout the region, but there was something strange about these. They seemed a little too predictable. They were almost square at the base. Nature doesn't produce square hills, let alone four of them. Finally, when we were nearly on top of them, I could see that they were set out in a giant square, with each hill forming a corner.

God

This was no accident. This was no random product of nature. This betrayed intelligence. This betrayed design. Someone had been here. Someone was responsible for these hills. I took my compass reading, got an exact bearing of latitude and longitude, and began making mental preparations for my return trip. Even though there wasn't much to go on, I was sure that intelligent life had produced those four square hills, and I intended to have a closer look. *That's* how I found that ancient city.

And that's how you find God.

Just as those four square hills only made sense if an ancient civilization put them there, so there are things that only make sense if there's a God. Where did the universe come from? A bubbling mass of mud at the center of the universe that exploded billions of years ago? If so, you must explain everything with the equation "Nothing + the impersonal + time + chance = everything and everyone there ever has been or ever will be."

And where did humanity come from? Where did our longing for immortality come from? Why do we yearn to know who we are, where we came from, why we're here, and where we're going when we die?

It takes as much faith to believe in the big bang and evolution as it does to believe in God. When I look down on the landscape of life, I see evidence of a Creator. I see design. I see intelligence. I see enough to make me say, "There must be a God!" If four mounds on the jungle floor whisper of an ancient Mayan city, then the universe shouts of a God.

And, of course, the overwhelming majority of people in the United States say they believe in God, but what do they mean? Fifty years ago in the United States, we would have gotten a pretty uniform answer. Today we wouldn't. Just as truth is relative in the eyes of most people, so is their concept of God. Each person feels free to decide for himself or herself who God is.

I read recently a perspective about God that's very common. "God is a very personal thing—which does not mean that He is a person. It means that each person has the opportunity to devise his own notion of what is God to him. That's sacred. None of us has the right to take that away from anyone else—which is to say that if we do, we are transgressing on something pretty heavy."[1]

This perspective is absurd. If there is a God, then no matter what *we* mean when we say "God," it has no real value unless *God* says the same thing. If there is a God, He is who He is regardless of what we think. *Trying to "wish" God into being what we want Him to be is nonsense.*

Who Is God?

God is an infinite, eternal spirit, creator of the universe and sovereign over it, unchangeable in His perfect character. The God we're talking about is the original being, the sole judge of all that is true and false, right and wrong, good and bad. He's the One who communicated to mankind generally in nature and specifically in the Bible. When we go to the Bible for a look at God, we find several things about who He is.

God Is a Trinity

In Lewis Carroll's *Through the Looking Glass,* Alice (of *Alice in Wonderland* fame) was asked to believe something impossible. Alice replied that "one can't believe impossible things!" The White Queen says that of course one could believe impossible things if one simply tried hard enough. She, herself, had made it a habit of believing six impossible things each day before breakfast.

The doctrine of the Trinity, that *there is one God who exists eternally in three Persons, one in substance yet three in subsistence,* is one of the central teachings of Christianity. Yet it is one of the most difficult to understand and one of the most frequently choked upon, for the simple reason that it seems impossible. One God exists in three Persons. Even to write it or read it, one stumbles over the mathematics. If something is one, it cannot be three. If something is three, it cannot be one.

Thomas Jefferson was a towering intellect, one of the most highly regarded minds in American history. As testimony to that fact, there's the story of President John Kennedy, who, when elected, gathered to the White House some of the most brilliant minds in America as a governing advisory team. At a state dinner with them, Kennedy said,

"This is the most impressive concentration of intelligence ever assembled at a White House dinner, with the possible exception of when Mr. Jefferson dined here alone." Well, Jefferson, with his massive intellect, struggled with the Trinity and once wrote:

> When we shall have done away with the incomprehensible jargon of the Trinitarian arithmetic, that three are one, and one is three; when we shall have knocked down the artificial scaffolding, reared to mask from view the very simple structure of Jesus; when, in short, we shall have unlearned everything which has been taught since his day, and got back to the pure and simple doctrines he inculcated, we shall then be truly and worthily his disciples.[2]

Despite such critics, however, the doctrine of the Trinity has stood for centuries as one of the fundamentals of the faith. Where did the doctrine come from? Why are we asked to believe something so seemingly contradictory? Asked with the right spirit, these are honest and appropriate questions. The word *Trinity* never occurs in the Bible, but we come to the reality of it simply by trying to be faithful to key passages of Scripture. To begin with, the Bible says in both the Old and New Testaments that there is only one God. In Deuteronomy 6:4–5, Moses declared, "Hear, O Israel! The LORD is our God, the LORD is one! And you shall love the LORD your God with all your heart and with all your soul and with all your might" (NASB). In 1 Corinthians 8:4 the apostle Paul wrote, "We know that there is no such thing as an idol in the world, and that there is no God but one" (NASB). So we have unambiguous statements in both testaments that there is one God.

Yet both Jesus and the Holy Spirit are also called *God*. In the Gospel of John 20:27–28, we read of Jesus meeting with His disciples after His resurrection. The apostle Thomas had been absent at an earlier postresurrection appearance of Jesus and asserted that, regardless of what the other apostles said, he would not believe Jesus had risen from the dead unless he could touch His very wounds. At this appearance, Jesus said to Thomas, "Reach here your finger, and see My hands; and reach here your hand, and put it into My side; and be not unbelieving, but believing." Thomas answered, and said to Him, "My Lord and my God!" (NASB).

Then we see in Acts 5:3–4 that a Christian named Ananias sold some land and gave part of the money to the church, but he claimed to have given all of it. Peter said, "Ananias, why has Satan filled your heart to lie to the Holy Spirit? . . . You have not lied to men, but to God" (NASB). Lying to the Holy Spirit was equated with lying to God.

In 2 Corinthians 13:14, we read one of Paul's benedictions: "The grace of the Lord Jesus Christ, and the love of God, and the communion of the Holy Spirit be with you all. Amen" (NKJV). This links the Father, Son, and Holy Spirit all in one breath.

So what do you do with this? One set of Scriptures says there is one God, and another says three different persons are God. You have two choices. You can get a pair of scissors and start whacking passages out of the Bible, or you can accept the historical doctrine of the Trinity.

Thomas Jefferson preferred the first approach. In fact, he created his own version of the Bible by cutting out the things he didn't think belonged there and pasting together everything he thought did, coming up with the "Jeffersonian Bible." I would rather trust the authors of the Bible. I believe in the Trinity. If a computer manual goes beyond my comprehension, it should come as no surprise to me that a divine truth might surpass my comprehension. Historic Christianity has held to the doctrine of the Trinity, and rightly so. There is one God eternally existing in three co-equal, co-eternal persons. Any other conclusion does violence to Scripture.

God Is Love

The Bible also teaches us what this trinitarian God is like. While we can't look at all His characteristics, we can look at some of the most prominent, the first being that God is love. This is no shallow love that characterizes so many human relationships but love beyond comprehension.

The story is told of a little girl who needed a blood transfusion. The only one who had compatible blood was her younger brother. The young boy's mother and father asked if he would be willing to give his blood to save his sister. He thought about it gravely for some time. Then he decided that he would. As he was lying in the hospital bed, donating a harmless pint of blood, he looked up to his parents and asked, "When do I die?" He thought he had to give *all* his blood and that it would kill him. Yet he was willing to do it anyway. That's a glimpse of the kind of love God has for us.

The Son of God came to earth, took on the form of human flesh as Jesus of Nazareth, and lived a life of rejection and suffering that culminated in His crucifixion. Though crucifixion was a ghastly way to die, Jesus was not the only one who was crucified. Many were.

But at the moment of His death, Jesus took on Himself all the sins of the world. Jesus "bore our sins in his body on the tree" (1 Pet. 2:24). This brought on Him an anguish no human being can experience or comprehend. Many theologians and Bible teachers agree that Jesus outsuffered any person who ever lived. Why did He do it? Because He loved us, and it was the only way He could help us.

A number of years ago, the USS *Pueblo,* a ship from the United States Navy, was hijacked by the North Korean military. The incident provoked a tense diplomatic and military standoff for a number of days. The eighty-two surviving crew members were taken into a period of brutal captivity. In one particular instance thirteen of the men were required to sit in a rigid manner around a table for hours. After several hours, the door was flung open, and a North Korean guard brutally beat the man in the first chair with the butt of his rifle. The next day, as each man sat at his assigned place, again the door was thrown open, and the man in the first chair was brutally beaten. On the third day, it happened again to the same man.

Knowing the man could not survive, the next day, another young sailor took his place. When the door was flung open, the guard automatically beat the new victim senseless. For weeks, a new man stepped forward each day to sit in that horrible chair, knowing full well what would happen. At last the guards gave up in exasperation. They were unable to overcome that kind of sacrificial love.

That's a prime example of what the Bible means when it says God loves us. He loves us with a sacrificial love, a love that applies what it has to our needs. Applying the analogy of the crew of the USS *Pueblo,* each of us is the man sitting in the first chair, but instead of merely getting a beating, we are to die. Knowing this, Jesus traded places with us, and when the door was flung open, He took the death blow intended for us. This is what the Bible means when it says, "God demonstrates His own love toward us, in that while we were still sinners, Christ died for us" (Rom. 5:8 NKJV).

God Is Holy

In addition to God's being love, He is also holy. In Isaiah 6, we read:

> In the year of King Uzziah's death, I saw the Lord sitting on a throne, lofty and exalted, with the train of His robe filling the temple. Seraphim stood above Him, each having six wings; with two he covered his face, and with two he covered his feet, and with two he flew. And one called out to another and said,
> "Holy, Holy, Holy, is the LORD of hosts,
> The whole earth is full of His glory."
> And the foundations of the thresholds trembled at the voice of him who called out, while the temple was filling with smoke. Then I said,
> "Woe is me, for I am ruined!
> Because I am a man of unclean lips,
> And I live among a people of unclean lips;
> For my eyes have seen the King, the LORD of hosts."
> (vv. 1–5 NASB)

In this vision of the Lord in the temple, God is high and lifted up. Smoke is filling the room. The whole temple, which was built to last the ages, shook as the angel spoke. It was a terrifying scene. Imagine yourself in the picture. What would you do? I would fall on my face and try to crawl into the nearest crack in the floor!

Have you ever seen the *Wizard of Oz?* Do you remember when Dorothy, the Scare Crow, Tin Man, and Lion finally got into the inner sanctum of the wizard? A great, booming voice filled the room. Fire and smoke from somewhere shot heavenward with great whooshing sounds. The four visitors were terrified.

Years ago, I was watching this movie with members of my extended family, and I will never forget my young nephew, gripped with fear, inching slowly into his father's lap while siblings and cousins gaped, bug-eyed, at the terrifying spectacle. I have often wondered if the movie producer had read this passage of Scripture before he envisioned the scene in the throne room of Oz.

My young nieces' and nephews' reaction to a television program is but a token of the response we would have had if we had actually seen God in the temple. We would all have turned to Jell-o statues.

Yes, God is holy. His holiness is a consuming fire. There is no evil in holiness, and holiness will tolerate no presence of evil. God, in the end, will therefore destroy all evil, all that isn't holy. It's a cause for terror to the one who has not been made holy by the work of grace through faith in Jesus Christ. To the one who has, however, it removes the sin and therefore the terror. The newly made holy one may call the Eternal Holy One "Abba," a term of endearment most closely translated "Daddy."

God Is Just

God's justice is something we hear little about these days. It's not a popular concept. We're living in a day when one of our highest values is personal independence. "I won't tell you how to live your life, and you don't tell me how to live mine. Agreed?" It's considered impolite and highly unacceptable to stick our noses into anyone else's business.

Nevertheless, justice stands as one of God's key characteristics. It can be defined as applying the consequences of a person's actions according to a fixed standard. The fixed standard says that if you take this action, this is the automatic consequence. It's applied without exception to all people.

God has said, "All have sinned, and come short of the glory of God" (Rom. 3:23 KJV), and that the "wages of sin is death" (Rom. 6:23 KJV). Therefore, God's justice requires that all die. However, God's mercy moves Him to provide a way of escape. God Himself, in the form of Jesus, came to earth and died for us so that if we believe in Him and receive Him personally as our Savior, God will count Jesus' death for ours, and we won't have to die spiritually. Therefore, since God has provided a way of escape from judgment that satisfies Him, when we accept that way of escape, God would be unjust *not* to save us.

When we put God's justice and mercy together, it destroys the two most common misconceptions about God. The first is that God is a celestial Santa Claus, winking and booming a cheery "Ho! Ho! Ho!" at our transgressions. Nothing could be further from the truth. He has fixed standards, and violating those standards brings fixed consequences.

The other misconception it destroys is that God is a harsh, unfeeling judge who is standing up in heaven, arms crossed, face in a scowl, foot tapping, heaving a sigh, just waiting for us to do something wrong so He can stomp on us like June bugs. Instead, He loves us and is very merciful. He wants us to be able to avoid His judgment.

These traits of love, holiness, and justice are only three of God's moral characteristics. He shares them with humanity. While we'll never experience the perfection of God in these areas, we can all be, to a degree, loving, holy, and just.

God has other characteristics, however, that we'll never share. It's like the large standard poodle, Sugar Bear, that my wife and I used to have. She was so intelligent we had to spell words we didn't want her to hear. On top of that, she had a runaway sanguine personality. Everywhere she went, she thought she was leading a parade.

As intelligent as she was, however, she was no match for a person. She would never be able to read the newspaper. She would never know the difference between Baroque and classical music. She would never understand the reasons for the rise and fall of communism. These things were beyond her, and there would never be any way to change that. But we loved her nevertheless, and she loved us.

So it is with God and us. There are things about God that go beyond us, and there will never be any way to change that. Yet we can love God, and He can love us. Let's look at some of those characteristics.

God

God Is Eternal

God is eternal, without a beginning or an end (see Ps. 90:2). If you're like me, it is easy to imagine being born and then living forever, but it's incomprehensible to imagine never having a beginning. God has always existed? It must be, but it can't be . . . but it must be. Not only does the Bible teach it, but logic demands it. Something must always have existed, or else something has come from nothing.

God Is Immutable

God has never changed and never will (see Heb. 13:8). That's what *immutable* means . . . "unchanging." Have you ever had to cope with someone who was always changing? It's unnerving, isn't it? You never know what to expect. You're never sure when you're pleasing this person and when you're irritating him or her. But we don't have to worry about that with God. He never changes. He's the same yesterday, today, and forever.

God Is Omnipresent

God is everywhere simultaneously (see Ps. 139:7–10). There's nowhere you can go that God is not there. That means you cannot be lost from God; you cannot be alone. No matter how lonely you feel for human companionship, God is always there.

God Is Omniscient

God knows all things, both actual and possible (see Ps. 139:1–4). There's not an act, a word, or thought that He doesn't know. This means you cannot sin without God's knowing it. It also means you can never get into any kind of trouble without His knowing it. And since He is everywhere, He's there to help.

God Is Omnipotent

God is all-powerful (see Job 42:2). He can do whatever He chooses. That means God is able to do whatever is necessary to save us, to keep us, to help us. If we're not getting the help we want, it's not because God can't help. It's because, in the mystery of His will, He hasn't chosen to change our circumstances. But in His love, He will see to it that His grace is sufficient for our needs.

Trusting God's Character and Abilities

If we truly believed these things about God, it would radically change our attitude and behavior toward Him. We are warmed by these thoughts as we read about them or hear them preached on Sunday morning, but let Monday morning come and there's a distinct shift in our thinking.

We find a memo in our box saying that someone younger, with less seniority in the company, has just been promoted ahead of us. We're now going to be working for that little jerk who isn't even dry behind the ears. Our stomach is pumped full of acid, our innards are injected with bile, and our heart is assaulted with adrenaline. We're angry, hurt, disappointed, and a little scared.

So where is God? Where is the steady direction of His will toward our welfare? That nice little Sunday-morning homily suddenly seems cold, distant, and not related to the real world. Merciful, is He? Does He know the young twerp we're going to have to work for now? Omniscient? Did He know this was coming? Omnipotent? Was He able to do anything about it? Love? Does He care about this situation?

You see, the problem isn't that we don't understand the attributes of God. It's that we have trouble reconciling them with the real world. If God is good, what happened to that job? Or what has happened to our marriage? What's happening to our kids? What's happening to our health?

So how do we keep practical faith in these characteristics on Monday morning? What does God have to say about that?

> The sufferings of this present time are not worthy to be compared with the glory that is to be revealed to us. (Rom. 8:18 NASB)

> Therefore we do not lose heart, but though our outer man is decaying, yet our inner man is being renewed day by day. For momentary light

affliction is producing for us an eternal weight of glory far beyond all comparison, while we look not at the things which are seen, but at the things which are not seen. For the things which are seen are temporal, but the things which are not seen are eternal. (2 Cor. 4:17–18 NASB)

In other words, God says, "I didn't promise you a rose garden in this life. I promised you a rose garden in the next life and enough grace in this one to see you through. I promised if you would dedicate your life to Me totally and live by My values, I would use you significantly in ministry to others and fill your life with peace, love, and joy. The problem is that you're living for this world, and you feel that I'm here to make your life comfortable. You think I have failed you if I don't give you the things you want or if I don't take away the things you don't want. You have things backward. You are to serve Me. I'm not to serve you."

We grind and chafe and labor through the things of this life because we have many things backward. We own nothing. We're owed nothing by God. Our payoff is not in this life. We have a job to do here, which is to manifest the character and proclaim the name of Jesus, to help as many others go to heaven as possible. We have a short-term objective. We can settle down and get comfortable later.

When we live for ourselves in this life, we're miserable and unfulfilled, even when we get many of the things we want. When we give up on this life and live for the next, we have peace and love and joy even when we don't get the things we would like to have.

God loves us. Always. He always directs His will toward our welfare. He is utterly constant. It's just that, from time to time, we forget which ball game we're in. As Jesus suffered, so we will suffer (see 1 Pet. 2:21). As God's grace was sufficient for Jesus, so it will be for us. We forget where we are. We're not home yet. We're still visitors on this planet.

I read one time of a missionary couple who had spent their entire lives in the Central African Republic, working among the nationals, treating them medically. Teaching them to read. Teaching them farming skills, building skills, and social and cultural skills. Sharing with them the gospel of Christ. When the time came for them to retire, they sailed home on a large passenger ship. It just so happened that Teddy

Roosevelt had been over in Africa on one of his famous safaris, and as the ship docked in the New York harbor, there was a band playing, crowds cheering, confetti flying, and banners waving. All this hoopla just over a president returning from a hunting trip!

It's not fair, thought the missionary. *The president goes hunting, is gone for a few weeks, and when he comes home, he receives a hero's welcome. We spend our entire lives in an underdeveloped country, forsaking comfort and recognition for the cause of Christ, and when we come home, there isn't even anyone at the dock to meet us.*

And then in a blinding flash of insight given by the Holy Spirit, another thought came into his mind: *Ah, yes, but the difference is, you are not home yet.*

You will be treated poorly in this life. You will not get the reward that is due you. That doesn't change one thing about who God is. It only means you are not home yet. So be steadfast, immovable, always abounding in the work of the Lord, knowing that your labor is not in vain in the Lord (see 1 Cor. 15:58).

Who Needs God?

So we have seen who God is; but so what? Who needs God? Why is it important to know God? In his book *Who Needs God?* Rabbi Harold Kushner has written:

[In my ministry,] I deal with bright, successful people, people I genuinely like and admire, and I sense that something is missing in their lives. There is a lack of rootedness, a sense of having to figure things out by themselves because the past cannot be trusted as their guide. Their celebrations, from their children's birthday parties to a daughter's wedding to a business milestone, can be lots of fun but rarely soar to the level of joy. And as they grow older, I suspect they either confront or actively hide from confronting the thought that "there must be more to life than this."

There is spiritual vacuum at the center of their lives, and their lives betray this lack of an organizing vision, a sense of "this is who I am and what my life is fundamentally about." Some look for that center in their work, and are disappointed when corporations choose not to repay the loyalty they demanded or when retirement leaves them feeling useless. Some try to find it in their families and don't understand why they are so hurt when adolescent children insist, "Let me lead my own life!" and adult children move to another state and call every other Sunday. There is a kind of nourishment our souls crave, even as our bodies need the right foods, sunshine, and exercise. Without that spiritual nourishment, our souls remain stunted and undeveloped.[3]

Who needs God? We all do. We need Him for many reasons. There *is* a kind of nourishment our souls crave, just as our physical bodies need nourishment. And without it, we wither and die. Saint Augustine, a third-century bishop and perhaps antiquity's greatest theologian, once wrote, "We were made for Thee, O God, and our souls are restless until they find their rest in Thee."

Hope in This Life

The first reason we need God is that we all need hope in this life. There are times when life overwhelms us, when circumstances and people take us beyond our capacity to cope. Perhaps we're facing an acute health crisis. Our life is hanging in the balance. The doctors don't know whether we're going to live or die. "Oh, God, help me," we cry instinctively at our moment of great need. Or perhaps we learn that we have cancer, and our challenge isn't to stay alive for that moment but to live for the next six months or six years with the sword of pain and death hanging always over our head.

Perhaps it's a financial calamity. Or perhaps it's not we who are in trouble but a loved one. A daughter is involved in drugs, or a son's family is tearing itself apart. When airplanes go down, when floodwaters come up, when we're faced with the calamities of life, we instinctively turn to God. We're driven to it. We long for hope, and at such times, only God can give such hope. Of course, many don't turn to Him even then. But those who do find that He offers strength, encouragement, comfort, and hope that can be found no other place.

Not only do we need God for the strength to face the challenges of this life, but we also need Him for guidance. God has given us the Scriptures, which are "truth." Jesus said, "You shall know the truth, and the truth shall make you free" (John 8:32 NKJV). If we don't know the truth, we'll live in bondage to our own selfish will, our misguided sense of right and wrong, and our genius for traveling north when south is the way we should go. There is much in the Bible that takes us 180 degrees in the opposite direction from our natural inclinations. We need the truth of the Bible and the work of God in our hearts to be led in the truth and to be free. We need God's guidance as well as His strength if we're to have hope in this life.

Hope for the Next Life

Another reason we need God is that we need hope for life after death. When I was a child, I used to go swimming at a nearby public beach with a high dive about thirty feet high. I used to watch the other kids dive off and thought nothing of it. *I can do that,* I said to myself. Some kids were afraid to go up, but not me. It looked simple. Exciting, even. One day, I began climbing up, saying subconsciously, *I'm not afraid. I'm not afraid.* And I wasn't.

But then I got to the top. I walked over to the edge of the platform and looked down. I was afraid. The thirty feet seemed like thirty miles! I nearly lost control of my bodily functions. I couldn't go back because there was a line of little lemmings on the ladder behind me, rushing to the sea, just as I was. It was one of life's most impossible moments. I couldn't go forward, I couldn't go backward, and I couldn't stay where I was. With cold hands of terror gripping me, I put my mind in neutral and jumped. I nearly lost my stomach. I nearly lost my eyelids. I nearly lost my bathing suit! But I survived, and I learned an important lesson: Things may look harmless when we're down on the ground, but get up in the air where we can see reality and it can be terrifying.

That's the way death is for most people without Christ. When we're down on the ground, young and healthy, we aren't scared. But let us get old or sick or seriously injured, let our lives be in peril, let us actually get up on the ladder, and it's a different story. We climb the ladder of life, saying to ourselves, *I'm not afraid. I'm not afraid.* But then we get up to the top, and we're afraid.

This fear is natural and God-given, because it's not safe to die without Him. It takes little insight into history, society, or our own hearts to realize that something is wrong with mankind. It's not that we can do no good. Clearly, we can. But we cannot keep from doing evil.

The Bible says all have sinned and come short of the glory of God (see Rom. 6:23). It also says the wages of this sin is spiritual death, or separation from God forever (see Rom. 3:23). Therefore, forgiveness of our sin and reconciliation with God is our greatest need. This reconciliation is not a complicated affair. In the third chapter of the Gospel of John, verse 16, we read, "For God so loved the world, that He gave His only begotten Son, that whoever believes in Him should not perish but have eternal life" (NKJV).

To believe, in the biblical sense, does not mean merely an intellectual acceptance of a given fact, but a personal commitment to it. To believe in Jesus means to accept in our hearts who He is and to place ourselves under His jurisdiction, to give our lives over sincerely to following Him. When we do, we see that God, in response to our faith in Jesus, gives us eternal life. If we want hope for the forgiveness of our sin and life after death, we all need God.

A Basis for Values

A number of years ago, I led several study tours to Israel and the Middle East. In Jerusalem, there's a museum dedicated to the Holocaust. As you walk through, you see artifacts on display that were taken from the concentration camps. Barbed wire, instruments of torture, and scientific equipment used in conducting human experiments on the Jews are all on display. In addition, there are pictures of the incomprehensible inhumanity that was inflicted upon the Jewish people in those camps. Skeletons with skin stretched tightly over them stand against barbed-wire barricades, staring out with hollow eyes betraying hollow souls.

The Holocaust stands as perhaps the most remarkable example of mass human cruelty in the history of mankind. It was an evil that everyone agrees was wrong. There are a million things Americans cannot agree on; we can't agree on abortion, capital punishment, or homosexuality. But one thing we *can* agree on: The Holocaust was wrong.

But why was it wrong? The Nazis were careful to pass laws sanctioning everything they did. So on what moral authority do we say the Holocaust was wrong? We can't appeal to law, because everything was legal. If we appeal to the universal outrage by saying, "Everyone agrees it was wrong," then what if everyone agreed it was right? Would it be right if 51 percent of the people said it was?

The reality is, if we can't appeal to a higher authority than man, we can't use the terms *right* and *wrong*. We can say we don't like the Holocaust. We can state that in our opinion it was cruel. But that's just our opinion.

One person says it's wrong to kill, and another says it's right. Who says which person is correct?

One person says it's wrong to be sexually immoral, and another says it's all right. Who says which one is correct?

One person says it's wrong to steal, and another says it's right. Who says which one is correct?

Terms like *right* and *wrong* can only be used if there's an obligatory moral base established by an authority higher than man. If we don't recognize God, there's no possibility of that moral base. It is as Dostoyevsky wrote in *The Brothers Karamazov:* "If there is no God, all things are permissible."

If we don't have right and wrong, it's very difficult to have social order. Not enough people agree on the same values to pass fair laws. And now, for example, in the United States, we cannot destroy habitat for the golden-cheeked warbler, a bird on the endangered species list, but we can abort a baby that's old enough to live outside the womb.

If we don't have a right and wrong, not only do we have difficulty agreeing on values for law and order, but we can't enforce the laws we do have. There are laws against stealing, but people on Wall Street steal with impunity because they can get away with it. We have laws against bribes and graft and kickbacks, but those crimes go on in business and government all the time. There are laws against drug abuse, driving while intoxicated, and pornography, yet those things go on all the time as well. The more people there are without a divine moral base, the greater the proliferation of self-destructive and socially destructive behavior. We can't sustain a democracy without a moral base, and we can't sustain a moral base without God. Morality must come from a higher level or it will sink to the lowest level.

If we need God, why don't more people give their lives to Him? The polls tell us the overwhelming majority of people in the United States believe in God, but their behavior is proof that they haven't given their lives to Him. One reason is that they don't *want* to give their lives to Him. If the God of the Bible exists, He requires things from us. If we want to find God, we must start our search for Him with hearts prepared for repentance and obedience. If there is a God, do we think we can tell *Him* what to do? No, He tells *us* what to do. And we must be ready to do it. The true barrier to knowing God is our will. The key to knowing Him is repentance and obedience.

Conclusion

I read a story once of a primitive tribe of people living in a remote part of the world. One day they saw footprints in the sand along their river. They were fearful and suspicious, and they kept their eyes open for more clues. Days passed, and they sometimes found food, trinkets, and knives hidden at the base of a tree or in a hole in the ground. As they continued their search, it led them upriver where, for the first time, they found some missionaries. They learned that it was these strange people who had left the gifts for them, and they were delighted that they had found the missionaries. They didn't realize until later that it was the missionaries who had found them.

So it is with God. When we find Him, we discover that it was He who found us. When we come to love Him, we discover that it was He who first loved us (see 1 John 4:19). Apart from God's grace, we don't desire to know Him. He gives us that desire (see John 6:44). He leads us in our search.

Do you want to know God? Or perhaps you know Him but want to know Him better. That's an exciting thing, an indication that God Himself, the Creator of the universe, is knocking on the door of *your* life. In a spirit of repentance and obedience, let Him in. Let Him into all the rooms in your life. Let Him clean out the sin, the corruption, and the selfishness in the living room of your heart, where your friends are; in the den where you watch television; in the kitchen where you eat and drink; in the study where you read; and in the bedroom where you sleep. Let Him replace the corruption and selfishness with love, righteousness, and holiness. He will do it. He wants it for you more than you want it for yourself. Give God all of yourself. Let the Master have His way. You've already demonstrated your inability to rule your life. Let the Good Shepherd guide you, protect you, and change you. Joy awaits when you do.

Personal Evaluation

Use the following exercise to develop your thinking a little further on your relationship with God:

1. What is the attribute of God you appreciate the most?

   _____

   Why?_____

2. What is it about God that is the most difficult for you to accept?

   Why?_____

3. In your own words, write a sentence or two answering the question, "Why do I need God?"

   _____

   _____

   _____

   _____

4. Perhaps another way to state the previous question is: "What is the difference in your life before you knew God and now that you know Him?"

   _____

   _____

   _____

In the Group

1. Begin this session by going around the circle and stating briefly what God means to you. Probably the best way to do this is to contrast what your life was like before you met the Lord with what your life is like now that you know Him.

2. People seem to struggle with the age-old question, "If God is a God of love, why is there so much sickness, disease, and murder in the world today?" Were you able to pick up any insights into this issue in your reading of this chapter?

3. God is immutable, omnipresent, omniscient, and omnipotent, among other characteristics. Pick one of those attributes and share with the group why that is important to you on a personal level and how this affects your life.

4. God gives us hope in the circumstances of this world and hope for eternal life in the next. Tell the group about a personal experience of yours where you have seen one of these two aspects come to life in your own world.

5.   When we find God we discover that it was He who found us. How did God find you? Is He still looking for you? If you feel comfortable doing so, share with the group your own story of finding God.

6.   Before the session is over, link hearts with your partner. Share with him any new prayer requests you might have and ask for an update in his life as well.

Memory Verse: "Before the mountains were brought forth, or ever thou hadst formed the earth and the world, even from everlasting to everlasting, thou art God" (Ps. 90:2 KJV).

Chapter Six

Jesus Christ

by Jeff VanVonderen

I CHEATED ON Life and Teachings of Jesus! It was a course I took back in 1973 when I was a student at Bethel College. The course required that we accumulate seventy hours of reading from various books about Christ. If we read the entire seventy hours' worth, we got an A on the reading report, which was 30 percent of the entire grade. Sixty hours earned a B, fifty a C, and so on.

The way I did it was simple. I would read a page out of one of the suggested books, time myself, multiply the amount of time by the number of pages, and write down the total (tweaking the number just enough to add for the "deep introspection" demanded by such vital material). I did this until the grand total equaled seventy hours.

At the time, I had what I thought were a couple of good reasons for doing this. First, this was a period in my life when I had a false god called "good grades." While in the most ultimate sense my value, my identity, and my very life were found in Christ, on a practical level I found these things in getting good grades, among other things.

Second, this was also a time in my life when I had very poor self-discipline. I had crashed and burned after several years of out-of-control rebellion. My study habits—and several other living skills—hadn't yet caught up to my new life in Christ. I had partied until the last week of the semester, which left one week for me to read seventy hours of reading. You can do the math on that one. Since I "had" to have good grades, and since I had seemingly left myself with no legitimate alternatives, cheating seemed like the only solution. When I turned in my reading report I received an A on it, which ensured that I got an A for the entire class.

When school let out for the summer, Dr. Stang, my instructor, got on a plane and went to Germany for a little over three months. It was only a little over a week before all of my "good" reasons for cheating disintegrated under the conviction of the Holy Spirit. I felt guilty and embarrassed. I grew increasingly miserable as the summer passed, dodging the well-deserved lightning bolts from the Guy in the sky whose "life and teachings" I had pillaged.

No matter how hard I tried to justify my actions the way I had originally, it became more and more difficult to escape one fact. What I had done was wrong, and I was going to have to talk to the professor. The problem was that he was in Europe, so I had to wait. By the end of August I was totally obsessed with the situation—I don't "do" miserable very well—so talking to him became my quest for the Holy Grail. "Indiana Max" would have been proud of my tenacity, if not my methods.

I found out which day Dr. Stang was returning and even learned his flight number and arrival time. I ferreted out his home address and calculated about how long it would take him to drive home from the airport. I even considered joining the Stalkers Union Local 356 (just kidding).

On the day of his return I telephoned his home. "Hello," came Dr. Stang's familiar voice. "Dr. Stang, this is Jeff VanVonderen. Boy, am I glad to reach you. I really need to talk with you. Can I come over?"

"Actually Jeff, I just now walked in the house." (*I did a pretty good job of stalking, eh? Timed his return home perfectly.*) "I haven't even said hello to my wife and kids yet. How about 3:00 P.M. tomorrow?"

I couldn't wait that long! "How about one o'clock?" I semi-pleaded.

"That would be fine," he replied patiently.

"Can you give me directions to your house?" I asked. (*Wasn't I disgusting?*)

The next day as I pulled up in his driveway, I felt like a man must feel who is going before a firing squad. Dr. Stang greeted me at the door, shaking my hand with gracious enthusiasm. *If only he knew what a sleaze I am,* I thought. Since the commercials tell us, "Never let 'em see you sweat," I nonchalantly tried to look him straight in the eyes. But I couldn't pull it off.

"I cheated on Life and Teachings of Jesus," I blurted out. Then I spilled my guts. I told him what I did, how I did it, why I did it, and what my summer had been like. "I feel so terrible about this, and I'm very sorry, Dr. Stang," I apologized.

Now, it turned out that he already knew ahead of time what I wanted to tell him. It seems that all kinds of people have cheated on that course through the years. He gets letters of confession from missionaries in Zanzibar ten years later who are thinking the reason they aren't winning any converts is because they cheated on Life and Teachings of Jesus!

Then something really bizarre happened. He looked at me with a smile and said, "Thank you for taking the time to talk to me about what you have done. I admire you for coming all the way over here to see me."

Silence.

"What!?" was the only word I could choke out.

"Well," he continued, "I think it took a lot of courage for you to come here, look me in the face, and take responsibility for cheating on my course. I appreciate your honesty. Thanks a lot."

"What?" I repeated. "Aren't you going to do anything to me?" I asked incredulously. "I'll do the reading, even extra reading. You can lower my grade, or better yet, flunk me. I'll take the class over." It all came out like a liturgy of heartfelt offers. For an exasperatingly long time I tried to talk him into accepting one of my offers, but to no avail. He just kept forgiving me.

After almost two hours he agreed to lower my grade by factoring in an F for the reading report. He said he was doing this because there was a scriptural principle he wanted me to know about: You reap what you sow. If you sow rutabaga seeds, you get rutabagas. If you sow immorality, you reap sexually transmitted diseases and broken relationships. If you sow cheating, you reap a bad grade (which, in my case, could have been worse)—and sometimes a lousy summer as well.

Why did it take him so long to lower my grade? Because there was another scriptural principle he wanted me to grasp. He refused to lower my grade until he knew that I knew that I could not pay for my sin. And I wanted to pay for it so desperately. You see, in the performance-based religious context where I was raised, I had learned that you can't feel finished or even forgiven about your sins—even your mistakes—until you have paid. The way to feeling better, even doing better, was to feel bad. In fact, some people can't feel "good" until they feel "bad."

"Choices cause ripples. Behaviors have consequences," Dr. Stang said that day. "Some people even experience the consequences of wrong choices for the rest of their lives. God has built the world that way, and it would be good for you to understand that. But He did this to help us have better lives and relationships, not to make us pay for what we've done. We *can't* pay for what we've done. In fact, it's too late! Jesus has already paid." Quite a lesson on the life and teachings of Jesus, huh?

Jesus Paid It All

First John 2:2 says, "He Himself is the propitiation for our sins, and not for ours only but also for the whole world" (NKJV). This is important because in Romans 3:23 the apostle Paul says, "For all have sinned and fall short of the glory of God" (NKJV). And in Romans 6:23 he makes it clear that "the wages of sin is death." (Death is what we deserve; it's what we have earned through our sin.) "But the [free] gift of God is eternal life in Christ Jesus our Lord" (NKJV). God's solution to our dilemma? A "forever life" package, purchased with the blood of Jesus and offered as a free gift to all who believe. Not a bad deal! Free life in exchange for earned death, all debts canceled. That's got the Home Shopping Network beat all to pieces. And that's what propitiation means.

The fact that a man named Jesus Christ lived, died, and rose again promises a lot of benefits to those who believe in and follow Him. As

I've shown, one of these is the satisfaction of the debt incurred and the punishment deserved because of our sins. There is no better case scenario than this. Hebrews 10:18 says, "Now where there is [forgiveness] of these, there is no longer an offering for sin" (NKJV). In other words, there's nothing we can do to improve upon what He's already done.

God's Man for the Job

A little later I'll talk about some of the other benefits accrued by those who have a relationship with Jesus. However, in order for us to relish them, indeed, for us to even have them, they'd have to be real. And for them to be real, Jesus had to be real. And He had to have the power and authority to procure and deliver them. He had to be God's Man for the job. So let's turn our attention to who Jesus really was and is.

Who Is Jesus Christ?

From a natural standpoint there is little question whether a man named Jesus Christ lived and died in Palestine about two thousand years ago. The most critical, nonreligious skeptic, when presented with the historical record, would probably even concede that point. There was really an Alexander the Great, really an Abraham Lincoln, really an Adolf Hitler, and really a Jesus Christ.

There is a huge difference, however, between this Man and those others—indeed, between Him and every other person who walked the planet. Again, from a natural standpoint, the existence of a difference, if not its significance, is acknowledged by many people in many ways. People don't base their calendars on the life and death of Lincoln. He may have gotten his own holiday, but he has to share it with George Washington, and then, it's only celebrated in the United States. Folks don't use Hitler's name in vain, as if he didn't have it coming. In Northern Ireland a cross, not an electric chair, hangs on the church of Protestants who shoot at Catholics and of the Catholics who shoot back.

But the *significance* of this difference is attested to by Scripture, by God, who inspired that Scripture, and by Jesus Himself. Millions of people have banked on its significance for deliverance of sin and guilt, for moral and spiritual transformation, and ultimately for their eternal well-being. Here is the important and remarkable difference: Jesus Christ is the personal self-revelation of God.

Jesus Christ Is God

Both Bruce Shelley and Max Anders have correctly asserted that the Bible is our bottom-line authority as believers. So what does the Bible say about Jesus? "In the beginning was the Word, and the Word was with God, and the Word was God," begins the Gospel of John. Who or what is this "Word" John is referring to? "And the Word became flesh and dwelt among us, and we beheld His glory, the glory as of the only begotten of the Father, full of grace and truth," John continues in verse 14 (NKJV). This very human Jesus, with whom the disciple John walked and talked, of whom John the Baptist bore witness, and through whom the invisible God delivered His truth and grace to humankind, was at the same time exactly God.

The apostle Paul agreed with this. Writing in Philippians 2:6 he said, "Who, although He existed in the form of God, did not regard equality with God a thing to be grasped, but emptied Himself . . . being made in the likeness of men" (NASB).*

The New Testament was originally written in the Greek language. How about a little Greek lesson? The Greek word translated "existed," which sounds like a past tense, is really in the present tense, or "the always now." Literally, this verse is saying, "He, who existing in the form of God . . ." Whenever it is now—which is always—Jesus exists as God. The book of Hebrews also agrees with this statement: "He is the radiance of His [God's] glory and the exact representation of His nature" (Heb. 1:3).

---

* Except where noted, Scripture quotations in this chapter after this point are from the New American Standard Bible (NASB).

That the man Jesus Christ agreed with this assessment can be seen in John 17:5, "And now, glorify Thou Me together with Thyself, Father, with the glory which I ever had with Thee before the world was." And in John 8:58, Jesus identifies Himself as God by saying, "Before Abraham was born, I am!" the phrase God Himself used to tell Moses His name in Exodus 3:14. There's no doubt that those who heard Jesus say this understood what He meant, either. They picked up stones to kill Him! Why? For claiming to be God.

Either Jesus was God in human form, or He was a great yet misunderstood philosopher and teacher. And if He was but a teacher, then His untimely death consigned Him to be only a flash in the pan at that. Behind door number one is Jesus, God intervening in the world to save it. Behind door number two is Jesus, one of the countless human victims of the world ruled by Rome. There are no other alternatives. Christians trust in the Jesus who is God, behind door number one, and by Him we are saved.

The revelation of God in Jesus Christ ultimately demonstrates that: (a) God is a personal being; if you want to see what that Person "looks" like, acts like, and cares about, look at Jesus. (b) God is love. Max Anders has already so eloquently discussed this point. The God who is love, without Jesus Christ, might still be God, but He is not the God who is love; and (c) God is person oriented. The Word became flesh because words aren't enough. Human beings need more than a relationship with inanimate objects or ideas. We need a relationship with other beings. Genesis 2:18 says, "It is not good for the man to be alone." The birth of Jesus Christ was God's ultimate assurance, "You are not alone."

More about Jesus Christ

Scripture says many other things about Jesus Christ. In addition to His deity, Scripture points out that:

* *He was born of a virgin.* God promised this in Isaiah 7:14: "Therefore the Lord Himself will give you a sign: Behold, a virgin will be with child and bear a son, and she will call His name Immanuel." There have been many people born to women who could not have children.

Sara gave birth to Isaac. Elizabeth gave birth to John the Baptist. But only one person was born of a virgin: Jesus Christ. When this happened, the world would know God had come through with His promise. That this did happen is affirmed in Matthew 1:25 and in the first two chapters of Luke.

  * *He lived a sinless life.* Hebrews 4:15 says, "For we do not have a high priest who cannot sympathize with our weaknesses, but one who has been tempted in all things as we are, yet without sin." Hebrews 7:26 says, "For it was fitting that we should have such a high priest, holy, innocent, undefiled, separated from sinners." And 2 Corinthians 5:21 says, "He made Him who knew no sin to be sin on our behalf, that we might become the righteousness of God in Him."

The word translated "sin" most often in the New Testament is the Greek word *hamartia.* It means "missing the mark." There are two important reasons why it is significant that Christ had no sin and never sinned. First, only a pure and sinless sacrifice could hit the mark as being sufficient to meet God's righteous requirement. In order for us to be rid of the sin that was ours and receive the righteousness that was His, He had to be totally righteous and without sin. This order was so tall, only God Himself could fill it. He did that in Christ. You see, Jesus was God's Man for the job. But He was also man's God for the job.

Second, Jesus' sinlessness is an example for those who follow. The fact is that Jesus Christ, the Man, constantly abided in His Father. Because He did this, He never missed the mark. "No one who abides in Him sins," we are told in 1 John 3:6. That is, "No one who is presently abiding in Him is presently sinning." It's already too late for us to duplicate Christ's sinlessness in terms of our attitudes and behaviors. We've already missed the mark. But we can seek to emulate His pattern of dependence upon and abiding in the Father. Each time we rely on Him to meet our needs, we won't be relying on people or things that can't meet our needs, things that miss the mark. This is the fight of faith. I'll talk more about this a little later.

  * *He performed many miracles.* Some miracles were "designed" to illustrate that He was God. In Matthew 9:2–8 Jesus healed a lame man "in order that you may know that the Son of Man has authority on

earth to forgive sins," something only God could do. Again, He was accused of blaspheming.

Some miracles illustrate that God unleashes His caring power in response to our faith. Matthew 9:18–33 describes how He healed several people "according to your faith." Some were healed simply to demonstrate that God supernaturally intervenes in our lives just because He loves us (see Matt. 9:35–36). The fact is that God was supernaturally at work in and through Jesus Christ. God's most spectacular miracle? The resurrection of Jesus from the dead.

* *He died and rose again.* God's intervention in human history is like a divine football game. In the beginning God carefully fashioned two human beings, and in doing so He also created relationships— among these two people and Himself—the kickoff. But mankind fumbled the return when we looked the wrong way, and the enemy scored. Unfortunately, it proved to be the only score the opposition needed because we were incapable of even moving the ball. God gave us a great playbook—the Scripture—but we didn't follow it. He sent in His best players—the prophets—with the plays, but we wouldn't listen. So God put Himself in the game and scored a ton of points. He did this with the birth, death, and resurrection of Jesus. In fact, so many points were scored that, while there was still more time on the clock, for all intents and purposes the game was over.

First Corinthians 15:3–4 says, "For I delivered to you as of first importance what I also received, that Christ died for our sins according to the Scriptures, and that He was buried, and that He was raised on the third day according to the Scriptures" (NASB).

We've already seen a little of why Christ's death is so significant. But what about His resurrection? Why is it so important that Christ was raised from the dead? Because if He wasn't, God lost. Can you believe that I once heard a rather famous preacher say, "The Christian life is the best deal around, even if Jesus didn't rise from the dead." That's not what Paul said. In 1 Corinthians 15:12–19 he said if Christ wasn't raised from the dead, death won. If He wasn't raised up, our hope is in vain, our faith is worthless, and our death is our end. If Christ wasn't raised from the dead, "we are of all men most to be pitied" (v. 19).

"But now," Paul continues in verse 20, "Christ has been raised from the dead, the first fruits of those who are asleep." The resurrection of Jesus Christ is like an incredible concept car, a model that actually exists to show us what the rest will be like. More of the same are on the way, yet in the meantime we're going to have to wait. A risen Jesus Christ is the first of many resurrections to come off of God's eternal assembly line. But more than this, Jesus' resurrection is the prototype of our own; it is another of God's assurances, "You are not alone . . . " He will never leave us alone. Not even in the grave!

* *He ascended into heaven.* Acts 1:9 says, "And after He had said these things, He was lifted up while they were looking on, and a cloud received Him out of their sight." Short and to the point. Jesus ascended into heaven. He had predicted this would happen—in John 14:3—and it did.

There are three important ramifications of Jesus' ascension. First, in heaven He is preparing a place for us to be with Him forever (John 14:2). Second, in heaven He is pleading our case with His Father. Revelation 12:10 says Satan is the accuser of the brethren, "who accuses them before our God day and night." But 1 John 2:1 reminds us that "we have an Advocate with the Father, Jesus Christ the righteous." Third, prior to Jesus' ascension, God was physically present with people (and not many) as a Man. After His ascension, God is present in people as God. In John 14:16–18 Jesus says, "And I will ask the Father, and He will give you another Helper, that He may be with you forever; that is the Spirit of truth . . . [whom] you know . . . because He abides with you, and will be *in* you. I will not leave you as orphans; I will come to you" (emphasis mine). So we find even in Christ's departure, not an abandonment, but yet another of the Father's "You are not alone" assurances.

* *He will return bodily to earth in power and glory.* Acts 1:9 showed that Jesus had been taken up into heaven. But that's not the end of the story. Verses 10 and 11 say, "And as they were gazing intently into the sky while He was departing, behold, two men in white clothing stood beside them; and they also said, 'Men of Galilee, why do you stand looking at the sky? This Jesus, who has been taken up from you into heaven, will come in just the same way as you have watched Him go into heaven.'" The return of Jesus is

God's cymbal crash at the end of His redemptive symphony, the ticker-tape parade after His blow-out victory.

Listen to the dramatic words of Paul in 1 Thessalonians 4:16, where he says, "For the Lord Himself will descend from heaven with a shout, with the voice of the archangel, and with the trumpet of God; and the dead in Christ shall rise first. Then we who are alive and remain shall be caught up together with them in the clouds to meet the Lord in the air, and thus we shall always be with the Lord. Therefore comfort one another with these words." How comforting it is, indeed, for those who belong to Him to know that someday our pain and struggles will be over. And how utterly frightening it is for those who reject Him. For them, eternity will be a permanently vacuous existence, devoid of the presence of God and any of the love that is His essence.

When will this happen? Neither humans nor angels know. Matthew 24:34 says only the Father knows. A lack of knowledge concerning the time of His return, however, in no way affects its certainty. In John 14:3 Jesus said, "If I go and prepare a place for you, I *will* come again, and receive you to Myself; that where I am, there you may be also" (emphasis mine). So while the Father has not disclosed the timing of Christ's second coming to anyone, the fact that it will happen has been disclosed, and everyone in the world will see it happen. We also know it is impending. Jesus indicated in the parables in Matthew 24 and 25 that we should live as if it could happen any moment—because it could.

What Does This Mean to Us?

So we have seen who Jesus is, what He's done, and what's in store for us. What does all this mean? In Philippians 1:21–23, Paul said that if he could choose between his earthly life or being with the Lord, he would choose to be with Jesus. But the fact of the matter is, he was still here on earth. And we're still here too. So what does this mean for us now? First and foremost, it means we need Jesus.

In Genesis 2:17, God told Adam that if He ate from the forbidden tree he would *muwth,* a Hebrew word that means he would surely and suddenly die. He and Eve ate from the tree, and they experienced spiritual death, which is separation from God, and they would one day experience the reality of physical death. Romans 5:12 says, "Death spread to all men, because all sinned." Ephesians 2:1 tells us that outside of a relationship with Christ we are "dead in our trespasses and sins." Death is the absence of life. Death is spiritual separation from God. Present and eternal spiritual death is the problem from which we must be saved.

Up to now we've seen a lot of facts about Jesus Christ, theological statements. I have felt reluctant to write them down. It's not that theology is bad. It's not even that it isn't important for us to be certain of the things we believe. It's that ideas and facts don't save anyone. Neither does agreeing with ideas or believing facts. James 2:19 says, "You believe that God is one. You do well; the demons also believe, and shudder." The demons themselves have the facts straight. And in John 5:39–40 Jesus said to those who even knew where to find the facts, "You search the Scriptures, because you think that in them you have eternal life; and it is these that bear witness of Me; and you are unwilling to come to Me, that you may have life."

"Come to Me, that you may have life." Correct theology about Jesus Christ doesn't save. The person of Jesus Christ saves.

Acts 4:12 says, "And there is salvation in no one else; for there is no other name under heaven that has been given among men, by which we must be saved." Life is found in a relationship with Jesus Christ. He said, "I am the bread of life. I am the resurrection and the life. I have come that you might have life." Life is what Jesus brings. In fact, Jesus doesn't just bring life, He *is* life. He said, "I *am* the way, the truth and *the life*." Why? Because without Him we don't and can't have life. We are dead. In order to be saved, in order to have life, we must get life from where life is. In Jesus Christ.

What about you? Are you alive in Christ? Place your faith and trust in Him, the One who died in your place, and receive His gift of eternal life. The most familiar verse in the Bible, John 3:16, says it all: "For God so loved the world that he gave his one and only son, that whoever believes in him shall not perish but have eternal life" (NIV).

For those who trust Jesus Christ as Savior, the benefits are innumerable. For us, being in a saving relationship with Jesus means:

* *We are completely forgiven.* What would it be like to be completely debt free? It wouldn't matter if you had incurred your debts intentionally or by accident, responsibly or irresponsibly. And not only would all of your present debts be gone, but all past and future ones as well. And every record that they ever existed would be destroyed. This is how forgiven we are because of Jesus.

Too good to be true? Look at Colossians 2:13–14. "And when you were dead in your transgressions . . . He made you alive together with Him, having forgiven us all our transgressions, having canceled out the certificate of debt consisting of decrees against us and which was hostile toward us; and He has taken it out of the way, having nailed it to the cross." The Greek word for transgressions is *paraptoma,* and it means "unintentional errors" and "willful offenses."

* *We are more than forgiven sinners.* We are free of our sin. Hebrews 10:12–14 says, "But He [Jesus], having offered one sacrifice for sins for all time, sat down at the right hand of God. . . . For by one offering He has perfected for all time those who are sanctified."

During the times of the Old Testament sacrifices, the priests would make daily offerings to cover the sins of the people (see Heb. 10:11). Once a year the high priest would go into the Holy of Holies and make another, more all-encompassing sacrifice (see Heb. 10:1). But he had to go back each year because those sacrifices merely covered people's sins; they didn't "make perfect those who draw near" (v. 1). In fact, each year's sacrifice was "a reminder of sins year by year" (v. 3).

In other words, the fact that the high priest had to go back next year meant that this year's sacrifice didn't do the job. But Jesus' sacrifice was once for all. And it not only paid for our sins, it completely removed them. John 1:29, speaking of John the Baptist, says, "The next day he saw Jesus coming to him, and said, 'Behold, the Lamb of God who *takes away* the sin of the world!'" (emphasis mine). We are so cleaned by the blood of Jesus "we have confidence to enter the holy place" (Heb. 10:19), a stunt that would have gotten us killed in Old Testament times!

* *We can rest.* I'll never forget my first day in the army. It was 1970. I was standing in the January drizzle, Kentucky's sad excuse for a snowstorm, with the other recruits at Fort Campbell. We were a pretty shaggy bunch. Many of us were graduates of the Age of Aquarius: "Give us a head of hair—long, beautiful hair!" had been our battle cry. I had just lit a cigarette when I heard the pronouncement that sent a chill down the backs of all us John Lennon wannabes. "All right, ladies. Load up the bus. It's time to get your hair cut." Bad rush. What a downer, man. I mean, I was really bummed. Oh, uh, sorry. I was having a flashback there.

Anyway, when we got to the barracks where the barber shop had been set up, most of us were in a pit of despair. So we were ecstatic at the news we received. There were three lengths of hair that were acceptable: two inches long on top, trimmed short on the neck and around the ears; a flattop; or a complete buzz cut. Most of us chose the longest alternative. Some picked the flattop. And some depressed souls had given up all hope of looking half human and picked the buzz. I was one of these. I thought, *What the heck. I'm going to be living with a bunch of guys for eight weeks. I don't want to look attractive. In fact, ugly's good.* I wasn't disappointed. When the sheering was completed, we filed back on the bus and headed for our company. The bus driver told us we were to muster immediately in front of our barracks. "You ladies are going to meet your drill sergeant," he taunted.

On the way out of the bus one of the other recruits said to the driver, "Hey, man, I thought that 'lady' stuff ended when we lost our locks."

"You'll need to get used to disappointment, gir-r-rls," he sneered.

It was a sorry-looking bunch of souls that lined up in the rain that day. Just as we were beginning to hope that maybe the worst was over, the driver's prediction came true. Out of the barracks marched Sergeant Kostansky. His face looked like a constipated Dick Butkus who had just sucked a lemon.

"Take off your hats," he barked. We all just kind of looked around. "Off!" he bellowed.

We removed our hats.

Then he removed his. On his head there was only the slightest hint of a five o'clock shadow where his hair used to be.

"Look at my hair!" he ordered. I looked, and I don't know about anyone else, but I couldn't see any.

"If your hair is any longer than this," he hissed in derision, "you are going to get it cut again." Sergeant Kostansky was a Jack Nicholson imitation on steroids.

It didn't take us very long to pick up on boot camp's predominant theme: Nothing was good enough. When we finished peeling the fifty pounds of potatoes we were assigned, we were given twenty more. When we completed the fifty push-ups we had been told to do, we were given twenty-five more. A mattress on the floor after breakfast told us that our bed-making mission had failed. I could see my face in my newly polished shoes—until the sergeant extinguished his cigarette on them and had me polish them over. We could never do enough well enough.

For a lot of believers, this is what the Christian life is like. Always trying, never enough. Striving to measure up to some spiritual standard but always falling short. Or meeting the standard and seeing it change. More giving, more church attendance, more serving, more Bible reading, more praying, but never enough. Many believers end up living the Christian life for the wrong reason, to earn God's "yes" with their behavior. Yet God's approval is already ours because of Jesus.

"There remains therefore a Sabbath rest for the people of God. For the one who has entered His rest has himself also rested from his works, as God did from His" says Hebrews 4:9–10. The writer of this passage was talking about the Sabbath rest that is ours as believers, and he used the creation to illustrate his point. God created for six days and rested on the seventh. Was He tired? No. Well, perhaps He was bored? Again, no. God rested on the seventh day because He was finished. He had done everything there was to do. There remains therefore an "it-is-finished" rest for the people of God.

This "rest" is not about the "whether's" or "what's" of the Christian life. *Whether* we live like Christians is not negotiable. Neither is *how* we live. This is about the *why*. Does it matter how we live? Absolutely! Does it matter whether we are to live like Christians? Yes! But we don't live our lives trying to earn or improve upon God's approval of us with our behavior. All that work has been accomplished by God Himself. We are able to rest in God's "yes" and live the life He desires just because we love Him. As 2 Corinthians 5:14 says, "For the love of Christ controls us."

* *We have a way through the problems and pain of life.* Imagine yourself on the crew of a huge frigate. Your sails are doused as you pick your way through the fog. Without warning the ship's bow makes a sickening groan, throwing you and your fellow crew members to the deck. You've run up on a reef! Water floods in below the deck as you start to break up. There's no hope of surviving unless you can get to land.

Suddenly, miraculously, your nostrils pick up a familiar scent as if from heaven itself. It has never smelled so sweet. Soil! Your hopes are confirmed as land birds materialize through the murk and join the circling sea gulls. But there is no land to be seen. Your salvation is there, with no way of getting to it.

A shuffling sound gets your attention. You turn to witness an incredible sight. A fellow crew member has tied one end of a long rope around his waist; suddenly he jumps overboard into the soupy brine. You watch in amazement as he swims into the bank of mist and out of sight. As the rope feeds out you call out, "Come back! You're going to die." But he keeps swimming. And then the rope gets taut, suspended between a mast and the now-invisible would-be deliverer. Suddenly a voice cuts through the mist. "I've found the land. Follow the rope. It will lead you to safety." You climb over the edge into the chill, and pull yourself along the rope through the watery path to salvation.

Actually, the Greeks really had a name for just such a person as our story's hero: *archegos.* And this word is used of Jesus four times in the Bible. Hebrews 2:10 says, "For it was fitting for Him [God], for whom are all things, and through whom are all things, in bringing many sons to glory, to perfect the author [*archegos*] of their salvation through sufferings." And Hebrews 12:2 says, "Fixing our eyes on Jesus, the author [*archegos*] and perfecter of faith, who for the joy set before Him endured the cross." Jesus suffered and died to secure our eternal well-being. But more than that, in doing it first, He made a way for us.

I remember in the early seventies, the church tried to counteract the influences of the drug culture by telling people to "Get high on

Jesus." But Jesus is not like some drug, dispensed by a Divine pusher to help mankind escape its problems and pain. Instead, Jesus has blazed a trail through sin, pain, and even death, to make a way for us to follow safely, by faith.

* *We have an Advocate.* Remember the Hebrews passage that said Jesus sat down at the right hand of the Father? Well, there's a story in Acts 7 about when Stephen was being stoned. Verse 55 says, "He gazed intently into heaven and saw the glory of God, and Jesus standing at the right hand of God." When it comes to His work of paying for and cleansing us of sin, it's completed, and He is sitting. But it's comforting to know that when Christians are in trouble, He is standing. Stephen, even in death, was so comforted by this that he could say of his murderers with his last breath, "Lord, do not hold this sin against them!"

Hebrews 7:25 says, "He always lives to make intercession for them." Some people live for the Super Bowl, others for their children or spouse, still others for their career. Jesus lives to intercede for us. Pleading our case before the Father makes His day. Why is it important for us to know this? Because the Father forgets? No. Because we forget. I want to always live for Jesus, but I don't. I try to always live for Jesus, yet I don't. In fact, at times it seems *I can't.* But even when I don't always live for Him, it is comforting to know that He always lives for me.

* *We have a new identity.* "Therefore if any man is in Christ," says 2 Corinthians 5:17, "He is a new creation; the old things passed away; behold, new things have come." What we have as believers is only part of the good news. Who we are is the rest. Without our relationship with Jesus, Romans 5 describes us as dead, helpless sinners who are enemies of God. That is who we *were.* But who we were is dead. "Our old self was crucified with Him," says Romans 6:6. Jesus Himself could not survive a crucifixion, and neither could our old selves.

We are not part-dead and part-alive, part-old and part-new spiritual mutations or hybrids with our new, spiritual part stuck on to us at salvation like some extra appendage. We are brand-new creations in Christ. I'm afraid the old hymn that says we are "Only a sinner saved by grace" is wrong. A sinner saved by grace is a new, alive saint! And we are not "only" anything. We used to be God's enemies (see Rom. 5:10); now we are His friends (see John 15:5 and James 2:23), at peace with Him (see Rom. 5:1). We used to be slaves, but now we are sons and heirs (see Gal. 4:7). We once were disenfranchised orphans, but not now. Now we are "a chosen race, a royal priesthood, a holy nation, a people for God's own possession. . . . You once were not a people, but now you are the people of God" (1 Pet. 2:9–10).

* *We have what we need to live godly, victorious lives.* Second Peter 1:3 tells us that "His divine power has granted to us everything pertaining to life and godliness." What do we lack when it comes to living godly lives? A fresh start? No, Christ's death and resurrection gave us that. An identity transplant? No, we have that. The presence and power of God's own Spirit? Nope. We've been given *everything!* Second Corinthians 9:8 says, "And God is able to make all grace abound to you, that always having all sufficiency in everything, you may have an abundance for every good deed."

Then what do we lack? Sometimes we lack faith. Second Peter goes on to tell us to apply "all diligence in your faith" (1:5). First Timothy 6:12 urges us to "Fight the good fight of faith." Galatians 2:20 says, "I have been crucified with Christ; and it is no longer I who live, but Christ lives in me; and the life which I now live in the flesh I live [not by trying hard to be a good guy, not by trying to live up to the standard, not by people-pleasing the religious crowd] by faith in the Son of God." Jesus was the *archegos* of our salvation, but He is also the perfecter of it (Phil. 1:6). Again, this, too, we receive by faith.

* *We have a great opportunity.* "We are ambassadors of Christ," Paul said in 2 Corinthians 5:20, fellow workers with Jesus (6:1), indeed, fellow workers with God (3:9). As agents of Christ, what message consumes us? What kind of God do we represent? When Jesus represented God, people beheld His essence, full of grace and truth. When the weary, heavy-laden, lost of the world, or even God's people, experience our spiritual agenda, are they left with a harder set of rules than the ones they already can't follow? Or do they come away with purer doctrines over which to feel "righter" than the next guy? Or have they seen a living testimony of grace, love, and acceptance, earned and settled because of Jesus and available as a gift?

This opportunity exists not just in our relationship with the world "out there" but also with those closest to us. As husbands, are we heads of our families like Jesus is the head of the church? We've spent quite a little time examining the kind of head Jesus is. Do we treat the lives of others as more important than our own? That's what it says about Jesus in Ephesians 5:23, 25. Or are we the head like the boss of some corporation whose bottom line is productivity?

And what about our kids? When my second daughter, Erin, was about two years old, she proudly presented me with a picture she had carefully colored with her crayons. It was unmistakably a drawing of a human being, yet there was great liberty in this picture—the guy had three eyes! There was also some writing scribbled in at the bottom. I noticed that the person in the picture was bald (which I am) and that the first two letters of the name were a J and an E. I wrongly assumed it was a picture of me, although I didn't quite understand the three-eyes business. I guess when you're two and looking up at a bald guy, the nose looks like it's right between the eyes.

Then I looked at the name below. *Jesus.* To Erin, Jesus looked like me. And I wondered if I looked like Him. Are we flesh-and-blood representatives of the God who gave His life to say, "You are not alone"? Or do our children always come second to work, sports, even church? Do I mirror a Jesus whose stance toward my kids is "Not good enough, unacceptable, try harder"? Or do I reiterate a message of unconditional love and unquestioning worth?

Conclusion

Back in 1985 I received a royalty check for a book I had written. I decided to surprise my wife for Christmas, fly us out to New York City, and take her to a Broadway play to see Dustin Hoffman. She's an actress and mime, and I knew my plan would be a winner.

We stayed in a hotel about ten blocks away from the theater, right near Park Avenue. During our walks, our rides in the taxis, and when we looked out our hotel window I noticed an incredible phenomenon. In this little section of town I saw paraplegics living in cardboard boxes and begging for money, people in thousand-dollar suits who probably run the world, and everyone in between. And I thought to myself, *The suits definitely have the edge here.* And do you know what? In every system that exists in anyplace in the world, somebody has the edge. Except for God's place.

No one has an edge in God's system. Romans 11:32 says, "For God has shut up all in disobedience that He might show mercy to all." This means that through His perfect and righteous requirements, God has set up a system where no one can qualify himself so that He can show mercy to everyone. No one can get next to God on the basis of his or her behavior, checkbook, position, or anything else. But everyone can come for free. God has leveled the playing field.

Do you have power, money, status? Is your family picture-perfect? Do you have a list of church-related activities from here to Houston? That still doesn't get you in the game. Are you broke, unemployed, unemployable? Has your marriage fallen apart? Have you run from God your whole life? Do you have a list of hideous sins that reaches from Houston back to here? You still can get in the game. Why? Because of who Jesus Christ is and what He has done. Won't you find your life in Him? Get life from where life is.

Jesus Christ.

Personal Evaluation

It goes without saying that Jesus Christ is the centerpiece of the Christian faith. After reading this chapter, it might be a good time to do a personal assessment of your own relationship with Christ. Use the following questions as a road map to direct you through your own personal journey with the Lord.

1. Have you accepted Jesus Christ as your Savior?
   Yes   No

2. If so, how long ago did this occur?

   _____

   _____

3. Where were you when you received Christ?

   _____

   _____

4. What were the circumstances that led to your decision?

   _____

   _____

   _____

   _____

5. If you have not yet accepted Christ, what is keeping you from making this decision?

   _____

   _____

   _____

6. If you haven't done so before, will you accept Christ as your Savior right now in the quietness of your own mind?
   Yes   No

In the Group

1. The story that opened this chapter was a wonderful illustration of a man forgiving another man of his wrongdoing. Have you ever had a similar experience where you did something wrong and then experienced incredible forgiveness? If you are comfortable doing so, share your story with the others in your group.

2. What difference does it make if someone doesn't believe that Jesus Christ is God? What difference does it make by believing He was born of a virgin? How about His death and resurrection? Is it essential to believe He is coming back?

3. What does it mean to you that Jesus Christ is our Advocate? What does that mean Christ is doing for us, even now? How does "intercession" come into play here? Can you share a personal illustration of a time when you actually felt these doctrinal truths come to life in your own experience?

4. What does it mean to you to have a "new identity" in Christ? Do your best to define that identity in practical terms. What are some ways you can begin to live consistently with who you already are and what you already have because of Jesus? What has been the most practical piece of encouragement you have ever received in order to live the Christian life? Why was it so helpful to you?

5. How did you respond to the story of little two-year-old Erin drawing a picture of Jesus that looked like her daddy? What does it mean to you to be Christ's ambassador here on earth? How do you best communicate Christ to little ones, especially if you are a father? What sorts of words and actions can pass on a Christlike image to a child? How about to older children? Teenagers? Fellow adults?

6. Join your prayer partner for a closing time of prayer. Find out how he is doing and ask, particularly, if there was anything in this chapter that was especially difficult for him to grasp or accept. Get an update on his prayer requests and then reverse the process: You talk to him about your situation.

Memory Verse: "In the beginning was the Word, and the Word was with God, and the Word was God. The Word became flesh and made his dwelling among us. We have seen his glory, the glory of the One and Only, who came from the Father, full of grace and truth" (John 1:1, 14 NIV).

ChapterSeven

The Holy Spirit

by Dr. Jack Hayford

THE MELLOW WARMTH of the spring Sunday afternoon was only one of many reasons Tom was in such a good mood, even though he was just then crawling out from under his '71 Ford. He patted the old car on the side affectionately, then wiped away the smudgeprint he'd just left with the rag he'd used to wipe his hands.

"That oughta keep ya' for another few months, Nellie," he smiled, now that he'd finished changing the oil in his "work car"—a not-yet-antique but aged four-door that made the daily nine-mile round trip to the lumber mill he supervised.

He had no sooner scooted out from under the car—having given everything one last check—and stretched his long arms to loosen a kink that had developed from working in the tight quarters underneath Nellie, when Laney came running across the yard. The five-year-old, arms extended like an airplane's wings, was emitting a buzzing sound as he dashed into the garage toward the kitchen door.

But suddenly, in one swift move, the boy was scooped from his "glide path." The buzzing, Laney's "engine noise" as he captained his imagined aircraft from thirty-five thousand feet through a sudden decent toward a resupply of foodstuffs (probably cookies), was instantly cut off.

"Gotcha, Champ!" Tom shouted as he swung the boy high toward the garage's rafters. At the same moment a squeal of mixed surprise and delight exploded from the human jetliner who had just been snagged by his father like a navy carrier slam-stops a fighter jet setting down on its deck.

"Hey, Dad—do it again!" the young pilot yelled as Tom flipped his son over and then stood him upright on the floor.

"Don't know if I can, Champ. That was quite a stunt, and I'm ready to quit out here. C'mon in, instead. Let's grab some milk and a bunch of those chocolate-chippers Mom just made."

Soon the dad and son had both finished washing their hands, and Tom was pouring two tall glasses to near the brim as Laney doled cookies out of the jar in the center of the breakfast-room table onto the plate his father had placed there for their feast. As he worked, the little guy looked pensive, his face wrinkled up with a twist that indicated a bewildering question was forthcoming.

"Dad," Laney said, "what's a spurt?"

"A what?" Tom queried.

"A *spurt*," the boy repeated slowly, respectfully enunciating the word to assure he was expressing it as clearly as he could.

His father repeated the word again. "A spurt?" Then, briefly analyzing his answer, he replied, "Well, Laney, a spurt is a kind of *squirt*—you know, like when you step on the hose and some of the water in it kinda jumps out at the end?"

The boy started to nod his understanding when Tom suddenly smiled and quickly interjected, "Hey, here's a better one. You remember at breakfast this morning when I was eating my grapefruit and some of the juice shot across the table and got you in the face!"

They both laughed. "Yeah, Dad—and it tasted good too!"

"Well, *that* was a *spurt*; that's probably about as good an explanation as you could get, son." The answer seemed to satisfy the boy.

Both were dunking cookies, and Tom was about to reach for the Sunday paper's sports section he'd left on the counter earlier when Laney, who had been quietly thinking for a moment, turned to his father again.

"Then Dad, what's a *holy* spurt?"

"A what?" This time his voice rose to a quizzical pitch. "Where did you hear something like that?"

"This morning, in Sunday school," the lad continued, his eyes inquiringly innocent. "Mr. Atkins said something about us learning to let the 'holy spurt' speak to us from the Bible."

Tom nearly sprayed milk and cookies across the room with an instant expulsion of unrestrainable laughter. He grabbed for one of the paper towels he'd laid out for napkins and smothered the volcanic eruption—nearly choking as he regained control. Then, having cleared the blockage, he simply leaned back in his chair, enjoying the rumblings of his own laughter. Laney watched his dad's spasms with that certain glee that shines from the eyes of a kid who may not know what or why but realizes he or she has said something cute or clever.

"What's the matter, Dad?" the boy laughed, mirroring his father's obvious merriment.

"Laney, that's a classic!" He was regaining control. "Listen, Son, I'm not making fun of *you*. It's just that you misunderstood what Charlie was saying."

He continued, "Mr. Atkins" (Tom and Julie taught their children to always refer to adults by their surnames) "was talking to you about the Holy *Spirit*. The word isn't *spurt*, but *spirit*."

"You mean like a ghost or something?"

"Well, yes, in a way. But, I'd like you to have a clearer idea than just 'ghosty stuff' when you ask about the *Holy* Spirit, son."

"What *is* the Holy Spirit, Dad?"

Tom slid his chair back up to the table and reached for another cookie, pointing for Laney to do the same. He was musing over what options he had to explain so challenging a concept as the Third Person of the Trinity to a five-year-old.

"Tell ya what, Champ. Let's finish these cookies first, then I'm gonna show you something I think will help."

A few minutes later, as Tom was rinsing the glasses and plate they'd used, he said, "Laney, get a pan out of the cupboard over by the range."

When the boy brought a small metal saucepan, Tom filled it with water then set it on the range and lighted the burner. He went on, "While I do one more thing, son, get me a few ice cubes from the freezer."

"Hey, Dad, are we doing some kind of experiment or somethin'?"

Tom smiled, "Not exactly an experiment—more like a picture lesson." As the ice cubes arrived at the kitchen counter, Tom placed beside them an ordinary cup of water he'd just filled from the tap.

"Now, Laney, this is gonna take about five minutes. But, if I can tell this as well as I remember it being told to me when I was a teenager at camp a few years ago, not only will you remember it for a long time, but you'll tell your son someday.

"First, you asked *what* is the Holy Spirit—and the beginning of the answer is that the Holy Spirit isn't a *what*; He's a *who*. In other words, the Holy Spirit, or the Spirit of God as we sometimes say, is a *Person*."

The boy's rapt gaze indicated he was understanding, and he nodded the fact to his father with a simple, "Okay."

"However, son, the toughest thing about trying to describe Almighty God—who made everything including us and who loves us so very much—is that He's so much *more* than we are."

"He sure is, Dad—I know that!"

"I know you do, but . . . ," Tom paused. "It's not just that He's 'more,' like more powerful or smarter or things like that. Beside that, He's much more in His very own being. Actually, God is three Persons in one."

The lad looked puzzled, his mouth unmoving but his eyes saying, "I don't get it."

"If that seems hard to understand, don't feel surprised, Laney. The greatest thinkers and the wisest men of all time have admitted that they don't completely understand the *bigness* of the Person or personality of God. But let's just say this: If God's big enough to be God, then as creatures of His we shouldn't be surprised if He's just a little more than we can understand."

"Then how can we know God, Dad? And what about the Holy spurt—I mean, *Spirit*?"

By this time the pan on the range was steaming, and Tom said, "That's exactly what I'm getting ready to show you. It's a simple picture, not only of the three Persons of the Godhead, but it helps show something about how each of them works in our interest."

"Godhead?" Laney questioned.

"That's the word for the 'whole team,' so to speak. There's *Father* God, the *Son* of God, and the *Spirit* of God—that is, the Holy Spirit." As Tom spoke, he took the cup, the bowl of ice cubes, and the steaming pan and set them on the counter. That he had the boy's total involvement was quickly confirmed when he responded, "I know who the *Son* of God is, Dad. It's Jesus; isn't that right?"

"Exactly, and just as Jesus our Savior is God, and just as the Father Almighty, our Creator, is God, so the Holy Spirit is God."

Then, pointing to the three items on the counter, he explained, "Here's the picture: First, there's the Father . . . " (He pointed to the cup filled with water.) "Second, there's the Son . . . " (He indicated the ice cubes.) "And then there's the Holy Spirit." As he indicated the latter, he added, "The steam rising here is what I want you to see as the *third* picture, Laney. Let me explain."

Just as he began, Kent, Tom's junior-high son, walked into the room. "Hey, Dad, I heard you saying something about the Holy Spirit, and it reminded me of something I meant to ask you the other day." Some of the kids at school have been arguing about the Holy Spirit.

"Come on in and join us, son—when I finish this thing I'm doing with Laney, I'd like to hear about it. It sounds like something your mom went through when she was in college."

The teenager nodded, "Hey, it looks like you're using that illustration of the Trinity we had in our class a few months ago."

"Then you've seen it? Great. Tell you what, Kent. Go ahead and explain to Laney what each form of water represents." Tom stepped aside, winking his welcome to his older boy.

"Well, hey, Laney, the key to this is in what Dad just said. Notice these three things—the water, the ice, and the steam are all the same thing. That's important to see—they're all the same *substance;* you know. They're all some form of water."

The five-year-old squinted thoughtfully for a moment, then said: "The ice is frozen water, the steam is from hot water, and the cup is just plain water."

"Got it," affirmed his brother. "Now, get this."

Taking the cup in hand he said, "Everything alive on our planet needs this *to live*. You know that, Laney. There isn't anything alive that can survive without water." Laney snapped a nod of agreement.

"Now *this* form of water kinda represents God the Father," Kent continued. "'Cause there's *no* life—absolutely *nothing* exists—that God didn't create. He's the Maker of all things, so like this water He's the Giver of all life." Then, taking one of the ice cubes in hand, he went on: "But here's a second picture of God."

Kent looked straight at his brother. "What's the main difference between the water in the cup and this?" he asked, handing the boy the cube.

"It's cold," Laney replied.

"Yeah, but that's not the point. Let me put it this way, Champ. We can take hold of the ice cube, but the water runs through our fingers."

"So?" The small boy seemed puzzled.

"So even though we can see the signs of God the Father's life-giving power flowing around us like a stream all over the world, it wasn't until Jesus came to us—God in human form as a man— that we could touch, feel, and see God." Kent paused, then continued: "Jesus—God in the flesh—came in a way we could really understand. He was touchable like the ice cube. That way He helped us sort of get a handle on God, you know, like *personally*." His emphasis on the "personally" seemed to get through to the lad, who answered a quick "Yep" to his brother's "Got it?"

Tom spoke. "That's perfect, Kent. Couldn't be clearer. But if it's okay with you, I'd like to pick up at this point because we're at the specific thing that got this conversation started. Laney asked me who the Holy Spirit is."

"Sure, Dad. Go ahead."

"Laney," Tom resumed, "the steam rising above this pan of heated water is intended to help us see how the Third Person of the Trinity works."

The child interrupted, "Dad, Kent said that word too. What's *Trinity?*"

"Right son. Trinity means 'three in one.' Like we said earlier—God is so *full* and so grand in His being there are *three* Persons. But remember, all are perfectly united as one and the same. Just like the cup, the ice, and the steam are all water—they're all the same, but each is shown in different ways."

"How's the Holy Spirit like steam?"

"Well, probably in two ways. First, just like steam is warm but you can't hold it in your hand, the Holy Spirit reveals the warmth of His presence even though we can't see Him."

"What do you mean by 'warmth of His presence'?"

"By 'warmth,' I guess I mean His *love* more than anything else. You know, son, the way you feel inside when you know someone really cares about you?"

"Yeah, you mean 'warm' like feeling hugged," Laney answered.

Tom smiled again. "Perfect! And that's what the Holy Spirit does, more than anything else. The Bible says the love of God is poured into our hearts by the Holy Spirit He has given to us" [see Rom. 5:5].

"In fact," the boys' father continued, "that's what Mr. Atkins meant today when he said we need the Holy Spirit to speak to us from the Bible. He was talking about the fact that part of what the Holy Spirit does is make the Word of God become alive; that is, warm to our hearts and filled with meaning to our minds. He helps us to *understand* God's love and teaches us to *live* in God's love."

Kent spoke. "You said there was a second way the steam was like the Holy Spirit."

"Right. That has to do with His *power.*" Tom turned his attention directly to Laney.

"Kent's already studied some of this stuff in school, Laney. But let me take just one more minute, and then we're done.

"Steam—heated water—is used in a lot of ways you don't understand yet, ways that accomplish all kinds of things that help us. It drives machines, it provides energy that ends up providing power for light—there're lots of ways heated water makes power."

"Ya mean like those big locomotives—the old-time trains they show on TV?"

"Hey, man," his dad chuckled, "you *do* know about steam and power. Right. That's the point." Laney smiled in response—feeling good about his insight.

Tom recognized he'd stretched the limits of a five-year-old's interest span. "So whatta ya say, Champ? How've we done on answering the question of who's the Holy Spirit?"

"Okay, I guess. I know He's God—and His work is to help me with God's love and power."

"That's good enough for now, son. In fact, that's *great!*" Then, with a light slap on the rump and a "Go ahead and play now" sendoff for Laney, Tom emptied the containers and began to dry and put them away.

We'll pick up on Tom and Kent's conversation later.

The Third Person of the Trinity

As homey and simple as the above exchange of an everyday Christian Dad and his two boys may be, it reveals two great facts about the Holy Spirit: His *mystery* and His *mightiness.*

From the mystery of His essence as third Person of the Trinity to the mystery of the way He works—unseen, yet warmly present—His grandeur as God defies full definition. Further, from the mightiness of His miraculous power to transform a human soul to the mightiness of His making God's Word come alive in promise and manifest grace, the Holy Spirit's power defies full description.

This is reasonable to accept. The fact that any facet of God's Person or work transcends our fullest grasp should never alarm us or excite doubt. Indeed, a God worthy of the titles of Ultimate Creator and Sustainer and Maker of the Universe, would logically exceed the full understanding of *any* of His creatures. Still, beyond the awesome fact of His transcendence, God has chosen to *reveal* Himself to mankind. The way He does this *always* involves some action of the Holy Spirit.

First, this is obviously true because, as we have already seen in the illustration above, the Holy Spirit *is* God: As with the Father and the Son, all Persons in the Three-in-One are perfectly united. So if God seeks to reveal Himself, the Holy Spirit is inevitably involved.

Second, even though the *unity* of the Godhead is a fact—each entirely of the same substance (deity)—it is also a fact that each member of the Trinity provides a *unique* expression of the Godhead. In His ministry of expressing the Godhead, the Holy Spirit works foremost as the *Revealer.* He does this in four ways: as the *Inspirer* of the Holy Scriptures, as the *Inseminator* producing the Incarnation, as the *Instructor* of mankind concerning the Person of Jesus Christ, and as the *Igniter* of new life in those who are open to receive Jesus Christ as Savior.

Inspirer of the Scriptures

The most tangible and abiding revelation of Himself that God has given to mankind is in the Bible—the holy Scriptures, which are the Word of God. There's no reason to be confused about where the Bible came from, because we are told exactly *how* the Bible came into being: the Holy Spirit produced it. He did this through human agents whom He inspired supernaturally.

> All scripture is given by inspiration of God. . . . For prophecy never came by the will of man, but holy men of God spoke as they were moved [carried along] by the Holy Spirit. (3 Tim. 3:16 and 2 Pet. 1:21 NKJV)*

It is the fact that God the Holy Spirit is the Giver of God's Word that both (a) establishes the authority of the Scriptures and (b) explains the vitality they contain. They are *given* by God, so they are absolute, final, and conclusive. And they are *breathed* by God, so they are filled with life, power, and grace.

It is in this regard that the Holy Spirit is called the Spirit of Truth. Jesus said, "When He, the Spirit of truth, has come, He will guide you into all truth. . . . He will tell you things to come" (John 16:13). Exactly how the Holy Spirit accomplishes this, giving us the full revelation of the Word of God in the Bible, is explained by the apostle Paul in 1 Corinthians 2:10–13:

> But God has revealed them to us through the Spirit. For the Spirit searches all things, yes, the deep things of God. For what man knows the things of a man except the spirit of the man which is in him? Even so no one knows the things of God except the Spirit of God. Now we have received, not the spirit of the world, but the Spirit who is from God, that

---

* Unless otherwise indicated Scripture quotations in this chapter after this point are from the New King James Version (NKJV) of the Bible.

we might know the things that have been freely given to us by God. These things we also speak, not in words which man's wisdom teaches but which the Holy Spirit teaches, comparing spiritual things with spiritual.

Let's take a closer look at these verses that show how the Holy Spirit transmitted the Scriptures:

* First, because He knows the perfect mind, thoughts, and will of the *whole* Godhead (v. 10–11), the Holy Spirit has given us words transcending human wisdom (v. 13a).

* Second, He has fully and freely disclosed the things God intends for us (v. 12b) by revealing these spiritual *insights* in spiritually inspired *words* contained in the Scriptures (vv. 12b, 13b).

Thus, the Bible is not constituted of human ideas but of God's ideas and will; the Holy Spirit gave it to us, *word perfect!* This is the reason wise believers make the Bible the absolute authority for all life, faith, and practice. It's also why God's Word should be honored as the plumb line by which all human insight or experience is to be measured. Always remember: *To honor the Word of God is to honor the Holy Spirit's intent for working in your life.*

Inseminator of the Incarnation

When the angel Gabriel announced to the virgin Mary that she was intended by God to be the human vehicle through which God's Son would be incarnated, she asked, "How can this be?" Obviously, as a virgin, the bearing of a child was beyond possibility.

There is nothing of carnal suggestiveness in the words that answered her query, but a holy word picture is given to us: "*The Holy Spirit . . . will overshadow you;* therefore, . . . that Holy One who is to be born will be called the Son of God" (Luke 2:35).

This "overshadowing," of course, did not involve intercourse as we know it, but the Holy Spirit of God *did* place the seed of life-giving capacity within Mary by the pure power of God. Paralleling the way *human* insemination brings *human* life into being, a miraculously *divine* level of insemination occurred that brought about the birth of the *divine* and *sinless* Son of God—made manifest to mankind by the power of the Holy Spirit.

Here then is the greatest revelation of God—Jesus Himself! So we see the Holy Spirit again at work as the Revealer, enabling the birth of Jesus Christ and thereby bringing the fullest and most complete disclosure of heaven's heart and will that mankind will ever see!

> The Word became flesh and dwelt among us, and we behold His glory, the glory of the only begotten of the Father, full of grace and truth. (John 1:14)

> For it is the God who commanded light to shine out of darkness, who has shone in our hearts to give the light of the knowledge of the glory of God in the face of Jesus Christ. (2 Cor. 4:6)

> Then Jesus said to them, "When you lift up the Son of Man, then you will know that I am He, and that I do nothing of Myself; but as My Father taught Me, I speak these things. And He who sent Me is with Me. The Father has not left Me alone, for I always do those things that please Him. . . .

> He who has seen Me has seen the Father. (John 8:28–29; 14:9)

In the light of this consummate display of God's glory as the Holy Spirit enabling the entry of God's Son into the world, always remember: *To open to Jesus Christ is to receive the greatest revelation you can know.*

Instructor to Mankind

Because of the *ultimate* significance of His work in revealing Jesus to mankind, the Holy Spirit works as the essential Instructor to mankind. His goal is to bring human beings to a knowledge and receptive understanding of who Jesus Christ, the Son of God, really is.

During the season of His earthly ministry, our Lord Jesus revealed three things: He perfectly unveiled (a) the *heart* of God for humankind, (b) the *will* of God for human fulfillment, and (c) the *power* of God for human redemption. But with the completion of His glorious ministry, His atoning death, and His mighty resurrection, Jesus returned to heaven. In order for a continuing revelation of the reality of the Savior to continue, heaven planned for the Holy Spirit to be sent to accomplish this. So prior to His ascension, and to prepare His disciples for the Holy Spirit's coming, Jesus explained how He would work. His words to them help us understand the Holy Spirit's work and His *nature*—that is, what His personal "style" is like.

Jesus began with His promise that the Father will "give you *another* Helper, that He may abide with you forever—the Spirit of truth" (John 14:16–17). Our Lord's specific word choice—*another*—is to be understood not as "different from" but as "another just the same as Me." In short, because Jesus the *Son* is perfectly One with the *Father* and the *Spirit,* there is no difference in the essence of Their being or character.

When Jesus told His disciples He would be leaving, they were dismayed. But His promise of another like Him brought comfort. Thus, there is nothing mysterious about what "style" we may expect of the Holy Spirit's ways or workings today. He will manifest Himself in ways that not only are *just like* Jesus' ways but also in ways that will still bring utmost glory to Christ, for Jesus said: "He will glorify Me, for He will take of what is Mine and declare it to you" (John 16:14).

Jesus also taught His disciples exactly what the Holy Spirit's *mission* would be and how they would become a part of it. First, He said the Holy Spirit would cause people to be drawn to Him—to Jesus Himself—as the testimony of His life and death was proclaimed.

> But when the Helper [Comforter] comes, whom I shall send to you from the Father, the Spirit of truth who proceeds from the Father, He will testify of Me. And you also will bear witness because you have been with Me from the beginning. (John 15:26–27)

Second, Jesus cited three specific things the Holy Spirit would do as *Instructor* to mankind—seeking to show the wonder of the Savior to our race, which is so tragically blinded by sin: "When He has come, He will convict the world of sin, and of righteousness, and of judgment." Read John 16:8–10 and see how Jesus explained this process:

a. The Holy Spirit convinces people of sin because without God's bringing us to a conviction of our need, our human blindness, pride, or self-justification will argue for our own self-sufficiency. *The Holy Spirit instructs us* of our need for a Savior because we are sinners.

b. The Holy Spirit convinces people of *righteousness,* of the fact that true righteousness is only available through Jesus Christ. He magnifies the truth of Christ's sinlessness and the perfection of His provision of salvation through the cross. *The Holy Spirit instructs us* that the answer to our need for a Savior is Jesus alone.

c. The Holy Spirit convinces people of *judgment,* that is, that all resistance or rebellion against God's Son and His Word will ultimately meet with eternal loss. *The Holy Spirit instructs us* that since Satan ("the ruler of this world"—v. 11) has been judged, the whole world is on a downward course of inevitable doom outside of salvation in Jesus Christ.

It is when this work of *awakening* the heart of man brings a repentance for and confession of sin—when the heart is *illumined* by the light of the Holy Spirit's revealing Jesus as the only means of salvation—that the fourth work of the Spirit occurs.

Igniter of New Life

To visit a mortuary and walk by the casket of a friend or relative is to be reminded again that there is nothing deader than death. Whatever cosmetic work may have been done and however well-fitting or familiar the clothes, there is *nothing* of the real person there—not really. People may say, "Didn't he do a good job!" in appreciation of the mortician's efforts at presenting the corpse, but no human enterprise can restore life.

And yet, when a man or woman receives the Holy Spirit's revelation of Jesus Christ, each one stands on the brink of the most supernatural experience a human being can have—*the new birth!* Though parallel in some ways, this event transcends in significance the phenomenon we would see if a dead body in the casket climbed out, fully alive! For a person to receive and experience the new birth, two basic things are required: an *admission* (by the person) and a *transmission* (by the Holy Spirit).

An Admission. When Jesus said, "You must be born again" (see John 3:3–5), He was pointing far above the shallow ideas of popular thought. Society uses the idea of being "born again" to describe anything from being resuscitated from a heart attack to having a near-death experience to finding a new career. (A public figure even once described his casual divorce and remarriage to a lover as his being "born again"!) But the true spiritual significance of the new birth Christ brings about needs to be distinguished from such humanistic ideas. Anything short of the *Holy Spirit's* work of a *new birth* through faith in Jesus Christ is nothing more than cosmetics on a corpse. The fact of death still remains.

The deadness of the unreborn human spirit is the result of our—all unregenerate humans'—being separated from God through sin. "The soul who sins shall die" (Ezek. 18:4 and 18:20). When God created humankind, He gave us a capacity for *complete* life as long as we would continue in relationship with Him. But sin and disobedience severed the life-support mechanism, as we might put it.

Just as a branch severed from a tree dries up and dies, so each of us—through our own sins—has cut off the branch we were standing on. Spiritually we are *both*—dead *and* apart from God—until we come back to Him through Jesus' cross. We come there for forgiveness, which is freely offered to repentant sinners (see Acts 13:38–39). Foundational to receiving the new life the Holy Spirit wants to lead us to through Jesus Christ is our admission of need and our confession of sin (see 1 John 1:5–10). So, I admit:

1. I am a sinner, dead and doomed through my own works. "For the wages of sin is death . . . [being] dead in trespasses and sins. . . . having no hope and without God in the world" (Rom. 6:23; Eph. 2:1, 12). Like the casket-bound corpse, we can do nothing for ourselves.
2. I can do nothing to bring about new life; only Jesus Christ can save me through the power of the Holy Spirit. Cosmetics or newly pressed clothes don't revive a corpse. The mortuary's commendable effort of "a good job"—still adds no life; and so it is that good works of ours can never save us: Only *Christ's* work is adequate.

Not by works of righteousness which we have done, but according to His mercy He saved us, through the washing of regeneration and renewing of the Holy Spirit, whom He poured out on us abundantly through Jesus Christ our Savior. (Titus 3:5–6)

A Transmission. The instant that living faith in Jesus Christ is exercised, the Holy Spirit works a wonder. He transmits the same dynamic power to us by which Jesus Himself was raised from the dead, igniting the power of eternal life within repentant sinners. This is called *regeneration,* for it is God's working a brand-new beginning at the center—the spiritual core—of a human being. Just as a car "out of gear" goes nowhere until the gears are engaged in the transmission, so "outside of Christ" we are dead in sin. It is the power of the Holy Spirit, engaging our lives—*gearing us with Christ*—that transmits *new* life and "gets us going." He brings us (a) into a life *for* Christ and (b) unto eternal life forever *with* Christ.

But if the Spirit of Him who raised Jesus from the dead dwells in you, He who raised Christ from the dead will also give life to your mortal bodies through His Spirit who dwells in you. (Rom. 8:11)

But God, who is rich in mercy, because of His great love with which He loved us, even when we were dead in trespasses, made us alive together with Christ (by grace you have been saved). . . . For by grace you have been saved through faith, and that not of yourselves; it is the gift of God. (Eph. 2:4–5, 8)

This *igniting* work of the Holy Spirit rounds out His work as Revealer because at this point He has accomplished the greatest miracle of all: *He has begun to create in and reveal through mere human beings the very life of Jesus Christ Himself!* This is the most incredible phenomenon in the universe. The literal resurrection of a human being—once eternally separated from God's originally intended purpose for his or her existence, helpless and hopelessly destined for sinful living and eternal judgment—is *now alive.* The *newborn* is forgiven of all sin, declared righteous before God in Christ, and now indwelt—literally infused with—the Spirit of Christ, who is now present to abide within us, with promised power to enable us to live and grow in Christ!

There is therefore now no condemnation to those who are in Christ Jesus. . . . For the law of the Spirit of life in Christ Jesus has made me free from the law of sin and death. (Rom. 8:1–2)

Therefore, if anyone is in Christ, he is a new creation; old things have passed away; behold, all things have become new. (2 Cor. 5:17)

This "new-creation" promise, transmitted by the breath and power of the Holy Spirit, introduces us to an entirely new potential in daily living. He comes to fill us completely and to do two things: (1) to reproduce the *character* of Jesus *in* us and (2) to manifest the dynamic *conduct* of Jesus *through* us.

So we have seen four ways in which the Holy Spirit is ceaselessly at work as the Revealer: (1) As the Inspirer of God's Word, He has provided us with a *perfect* revelation in the Scriptures. (2) As the Inseminator of the Incarnation, He has provided us with the *ultimate* revelation of Christ—God present among us in the flesh. (3) As the Instructor of mankind, He is providing a *spreading* revelation of the Gospel—magnifying Christ and drawing the lost to Him. (4) As the Igniter of new life, He is resurrecting unto eternal life those who receive Jesus Christ and bringing all of the *forgiven* to the promise of the *fullness* of Christ. "Christ in you, the hope of glory," the Bible says (Col. 1:27), describing the new life power indwelling believers by the work of the Holy Spirit.

But once He completes His work of revealing God's Word, His will, and His Son *to* us, the next thing the Holy Spirit wants to do is begin to reveal Christ *through* us. Having come to *know* Christ, we're called to *show* Christ. How?

Jesus emphasized that He would provide the Holy Spirit's power as an empowering resource to *everyone* who believes on Him. He put it in glorious and dynamic words:

> "He who believes in Me, as the Scripture has said, out of his inner being will flow rivers of living water." But this He spoke concerning the Spirit, whom those believing in Him would receive; for the Holy Spirit was not yet given, because Jesus was not yet glorified. (John 7:38–39)

It is here that the *possibilities* of the Holy Spirit's fullness are assured to us all in Christ. But we need to actively *participate* in His promise.

Jesus made clear that Spirit-fullness is no passive matter. He showed how the Holy Spirit, who indwells or initially fills us as believers, desires to *overflow us,* that He wants to continuously expand and spread the testimony of God's love and power given to us in His Son. For that to occur—as overflowing *rivers* of living water—we need to be *active* in our response to His presence. We need to learn a way of life *in* the Holy Spirit, just as surely as we have been brought to life *by* the Holy Spirit.

* * *

Tom and Kent had just returned from the track at the high school four blocks away. Their time of jogging together—which Tom had suggested "to burn off the cookie calories"—hadn't afforded a good time to pursue his oldest son's question, but as the two finished toweling down and started dressing following their shower, he reopened the earlier talk.

"You know," Tom began, reaching over to pat the teenager's back, "that was really great the way you explained the Trinity to Laney today. I was really proud of you."

Kent was buttoning his shirt, and it was clear his father's words and gesture registered their intended affirmation. He grinned. "Thanks, Dad; it was neat. I surprised myself—remembered the stuff better than I would have guessed I could. Is this a good time to talk about that argument at school?"

Just then, Julie called down the hall.

"How are the grown gentlemen of my life feeling? You guys want a sandwich or something before church? We'll need to leave in about an hour." Since it was Sunday, the main meal had been earlier, and as the grandfather clock punctuated his wife's inquiry at 4:30, Tom's stomach confirmed his ready appetite. He glanced at Kent, whose "thumbs-up" signaled a "go" on the snack.

"Sure enough, Honey! Five minutes, okay?"

"Fine. I'm gonna slice up some of the meatloaf left over from Friday."

The father and son had already launched their conversation by the time Julie signaled them from the den to the breakfast-room table.

"Sounds like you two are solving church history's theological problems pretty efficiently," she said. Having overheard the whole exchange, she summarized, "So some kids at school from Our Savior's Church were a little starchy about varying views concerning the Holy Spirit's work and ministry?"

Kent's shoulders shrugged his response, reflecting his sense of bewilderment, and Tom answered. "Yeah, you know the old story pretty well, Hon. I was just explaining to Kent that the most important thing is to keep perspective of the central issue: The Holy Spirit is here to glorify Jesus, not to verify us, and He's grieved when debate substitutes for love or when doctrinal issues are forged into swords for infighting rather than the truth of God's Word being used as an instrument against the devil."

"Dad said you had something like this happen to you, too, when you were in college, Mom. You were confronted about your beliefs?"

She slid onto the empty chair beside her husband, across from her son: "Yes—and in fact, it's actually become a happy memory because it settled a major issue for both your dad and me."

"Go ahead, Babe," Tom prodded. "We've got time."

"Well, son, our campus fellowship started to divide over the question of what it means to be filled with the Holy Spirit. I heard you and Dad in the den and could tell that that's the same thing the argument at your school was about.

"First of all, it's certainly a worthwhile question—because we all *need* the Spirit's power: for daily wisdom, to flavor our living, to inspire our service, and to keep an edge on our witness."

"Hey, wait a minute, Mom. That's good." The junior-higher grabbed the notepad from the counter by the telephone and started scrawling rapidly. "Say those four things again."

Julie looked at Tom, amused with herself: "What did I say, Honey? Must've been gems." She smiled.

"It *was* good, Hon. Let's see, you said the Holy Spirit's power is to give us wisdom, to inspire service, to enable our witness . . . ," he paused.

"And there was something about flavoring," Kent added.

"To flavor our *living*, I think I said," his mother stated reflectively.

"Right! This is *great!*" the boy exuded, "I've got what I need for my talk."

"What talk is that?" Julie asked. Tom's face indicated he too was unaware of what their son was referencing.

"Next week," Kent answered. "I'm one of three in the youth group who have been assigned to speak for four minutes on the theme, 'Why I want to be and stay filled with the Holy Spirit.'"

"I'm glad to know that, Kent. You'll do well—and I can certainly see why the subject is on your mind." She reached across the table, gave his hand a gentle touch, then pointed to the notepad: "You're excited about *my* accidental four-point outline, but let me tell you how excited I am about what *you* just said."

"What's that?"

"The exact wording of your subject includes the key your Dad and I learned—the one we think answers the question that often divides good Christians on the subject of the Holy Spirit.

"When we focus on why we want to be and stay filled" (she gestured as well as intoned her emphasis on the two verbs), "we feel we basically remove divisive issues about Holy Spirit fullness."

Tom spoke up. "That's right, son. Your mother and I found that whatever differences people had on the *doctrinal* questions of *when* or *how* a person is filled with the Holy Spirit or about *what happens* when he or she is filled, in the long run aren't the most important issues."

"Well, that's the stuff those kids were pushin' me on at school. They're good guys, but they were kinda gettin' on my case because they said our church is different from theirs."

"In what way?" his Mom inquired.

"On those exact things you were just sayin'—when, how, and what happens."

"Then, Kent, it's good to be clear on what the real bottom line is," Julie replied. "The *real* question for each of us is to inquire of *ourselves*, not to debate with one another, whether we are fully open to, yielded under, and being filled with the Holy Spirit *today*."

"Say it again, Mom." The boy leaned over the notepad again.

"Are we *open to* . . ." She waited as he wrote. "*Yielded under* . . . and *being filled with* the Holy Spirit—*today*?" She emphasized the last word. Then, after the teenager wrote it, she reached for the pad and pencil and inscribed a huge exclamation point after "today" before returning it to her son with a smile. "That's the *real* issue, son: *today!*"

Tom had just stood up, and he beckoned to Kent. "We've got to get ready to leave in a few minutes; let's finish this off over at the sink." Julie left the room to get ready for church, calling to Laney to do the same.

"Looks like this is becoming our theology lab," he chuckled. "First with Laney, now here we are again. Just let me illustrate something real quick and simple."

He had put a glass in the sink and was filling it with water. When it was full to the brim, he turned off the water.

"First, let me explain: The glass is you, me, or anyone else who has received Jesus as his or her Savior. The water is the Holy Spirit, and as you can see, the glass is full of the water.

"Now, I'm gonna bypass the question of differences on how and when the glass gets filled. As you may know, some Christians make a difference in when and how they feel this occurs."

"Yeah," Kent responded, "and that's what was so sticky when the kids from Our Savior's were talking to Kendra and me about this."

"Kendra was there too?" Kendra was Kent's eleventh-grade sister, Tom and Julie's oldest child and only daughter.

"Yeah, she pulled up in the car to take me home after school."

"What did she say?"

"She said that she respected their feelings and wanted them to know that even if we saw the how and the when differently, it didn't affect our feelings as to how much they love Jesus or how good of Christians they are. She kinda closed it off without being mean or anything, saying something like, 'We sure don't feel better than you for our approach to Holy Spirit fullness.'"

"Good," Tom said. "Mom and I had a talk like this with her quite awhile back. I'm glad she handled it that way." He turned back to the sink, resuming. "Now, look here. If that glass—filled to the brim—was sitting outside in the sun for long, what would happen?"

"Uh—wait, I remember the word . . . uh— *dehydrate!*" The boy was pleased with himself. "It would gradually empty, 'cause the sunlight kinda dries it out."

"Correct. The dehydration evaporates the water—that's the drying out you mentioned." Tom turned the tap again to a gentle rate of outflow. "Now, if this water was turned on—even if the glass was in the sun—what would happen?"

"No problem," he breezed. "The water pouring in would keep it full all the time—in fact, overflowing!"

"Bingo, buddy!" Tom laughed. "Overflowing is the key. It's *everything,* in fact." He motioned back to their chairs at the table.

"To wrap it up, Kent, listen to this one passage." The boy's dad took his Bible, which had just been laid there by Julie as she started to gather her brood. He scooted his chair beside Kent's. "Here it is, Ephesians 5:17–21: 'Therefore do not be unwise, but understand what the will of the Lord is. And do not be drunk with wine, in which is dissipation; but be filled with the Spirit, speaking to one another in psalms and hymns and spiritual songs, singing and making melody in your heart to the Lord, giving thanks always for all things to God the Father in the name of our Lord Jesus Christ, submitting to one another in the fear of God.'

"There are a lotta great things to say about this passage, son, but I just want to explain one thing right now. It's this phrase, in verse 18, 'be filled with the Spirit.'

"In a Bible study a long time ago, when Mom and I were in that college group, we learned that the Greek text in this passage literally says, 'Keep on being filled with the Spirit!' It's a *command,* and it calls every Christian to *continuous* refillings with the Holy Spirit."

"Continuous refillings? Is that like a bunch of experiences?"

"Well, what did you see in the sink?"

"You mean when the water kept running?"

"Yeah."

"Well, the glass just stayed full all the time—in fact, it was over-flowing."

"And that's the idea in this verse. We're pointed toward *staying* full. Just as the sun dehydrates the glass of water, the heat of daily circumstance will drain any one of us of spiritual energy—unless we 'keep on being filled with the Spirit.'"

"So that's why you and Mom decided the issue isn't when or how someone's filled, but that we're full *now.*"

"Exactly," Tom answered. "But remember, there's a command that calls for our obedience and response.

"In other words, since you and I aren't glasses—but each of us is an individual with an individual mind, attitudes, and pursuits—we each have to decide for *ourselves*—often, many times a day, *Am I willing to stay under the faucet?* if you know what I mean."

"I do, Dad." Kent paused, pensively—then looked at the notepad still there on the table. "You're saying we need to—as Mom put it—stay *open to, yielded under,* and *being filled with* the Holy Spirit—*today!*"

As the teenage boy emphasized "today," miming his mother's earlier emphasis, and as his dad nodded agreement, they grinned at each other. The conversation completed, Tom struck a light punch on his son's arm, saying "C'mon, guy, it's church time!" And the two men started for the door, Bibles in hand.

The Mission of the Holy Spirit

A study of the Holy Spirit is never complete until His ministry *in* and *through* each believer is understood. His central mission, to glorify Christ and bring mankind to salvation, is achieved by one means only—through His filling of human agents—people like you and me—with spiritual power.

The equipping of mere human beings for so supernatural a task as bringing other humans (1) unto belief in an *unseen* God, (2) unto faith in the words of an *ancient* Book, and (3) unto a humble trust and commitment to an *invisible* Savior who (4) is reported to be alive today, *requires miracle-working power!* Think of it: Operating by a dynamic that exceeds even the finest human persuasiveness, the Spirit of God does exactly that. As the apostle Paul said to a group of believers he had led to Christ,

> My speech and my preaching were not with persuasive words of human wisdom, but in the demonstration of the Spirit and of power, that your faith should not be in the wisdom of men but in the power of God. (1 Cor. 2:4–5)

To accomplish this "equipping" of us believers, the Holy Spirit fills us with His power for two purposes: to develop *credible* and *capacitated* witnesses. This means He makes us *believable as people* and *able as communicators,* extending the love of God and the testimony of Jesus. He can do this in *us.*

The Holy Spirit can establish a new credibility in us by the way He cultivates the *character* of Jesus Christ in our *living.* He can also engender in us a new capability as He reveals Christ's words and works *through* us, generating His supernatural love and power by anointing our *serving.* Let's elaborate on these two truths.

The Character of Christ: Living Reality

One of the most convincing evidences of the truth of the gospel is its power to transform the human personality. Once we have received Christ, the Holy Spirit immediately goes to work to begin reproducing in us the qualities of Jesus Himself—His traits, His graciousness, His character.

This work or process is called *sanctification,* a word that means the Holy Spirit is making us Christ's own. He is "setting us apart" as instruments or tools for the purpose and use of our Father and His Son Jesus.

The incredible power of the Holy Spirit to bring about mammoth change in us—even the most sinful of us—is testified to in Paul's words to the Corinthians. Notice his list of the lifestyles of these new believers *before* they knew Christ: fornicators, idolaters, adulterers, homosexuals, sodomites, thieves, insatiable addicts, drunkards, arguers, cheaters (see 1 Cor. 6:9–10).

But in contrast to their past, Paul seems to shout the glory of God's power seen in the *present* transformation of these sinners by His Holy Spirit: "And such were some of you. But you were washed [in Christ's blood], but you were sanctified [by the power of the Holy Spirit], but you were justified [declared righteous through the cross] in the name of the Lord Jesus and by the Spirit of our God" (1 Cor. 6:11).

This new quality of character is something God's Spirit grows from within us; that's why it's called "the fruit of the Holy Spirit." To dramatize its distinct beauty, this "fruit" that He is able to produce in us is set opposite "the works of the flesh" in Galatians 5:19–25. Because we are all capable of reverting to our old, sinful natures, a look at the stark difference between the two is a strong motivation for us all to stay filled with the Holy Spirit.

> Now the works of the flesh are evident, which are: adultery, fornication, uncleanness, lewdness, idolatry, sorcery, hatred, contentions, jealousies, outbursts of wrath, selfish ambitions, dissensions, heresies, envy, murders, drunkenness, revelries, and the like; of which I tell you beforehand, just as I also told you in time past, that those who practice such things will not inherit the kingdom of God.
>
> But the fruit of the Spirit is love, joy, peace, longsuffering, kindness, goodness, faithfulness, gentleness, self-control. Against such there is no law. And those who are Christ's have crucified the flesh with its passions and desires. If we live in the Spirit, let us also walk in the Spirit. (Gal. 5:19–25)

So we see how we're called to welcome the work of the Holy Spirit to cultivate Jesus' character and mind-set in us. His objective is more than simply producing *purity* in us. He wants to show the *credibility* of Christ's life *in* us—to give weight to our witness *about* Him.

Just as we are learning to *live* Christ, we are also called to *give* Christ. The Holy Spirit makes this possible too.

The Conduct of Christ: Life-giving Vitality

By "conduct," we most frequently think of behavior, and Christlike character will cultivate that. But we're using conduct here in a more expansive way—as with a *transmitting* of something from one place or person to another. Just as a tour guide, or conductor, helps people find their way on a tour, the Holy Spirit wants to make us conductors—indeed, He wants us to consider the possibility of becoming *superconductors!* Let me explain.

Recent work in the science of physics has opened the way to enabling the release of greater energy than ever from atomic particles. The key has been through learning the development and use of superconductors. Since the development of these devices, researchers have found a way to generate energy *twenty times greater* than ever before! Knowing how it is produced isn't necessary to understand this illustration, but the definition of what makes a superconductor possible holds a powerful insight. Listen to it: "A material is considered a superconductor when it loses all resistance to the flow of electricity."

What a lesson! Here is energy released to miraculously new dimensions that were impossible before, all because unintended but nonetheless present resistance is neutralized. What an insight into ourselves! How often our weakness, doubt, fear, or unbelief—our proud, self-seeking, or carnal ways—obstruct the Holy Spirit's pure release of Christ's power. We may not intend to resist, but we end up as a *clog* in the conduit rather than as a *conductor* of God's power. Still, the Holy Spirit can change that by working in us, and that possibility may well evoke our prayer: "O Lord, let me learn to yield under Your hand; to cease all resistance to the flow of Your Holy Spirit's power, to *live* according to Your Word, to *abide* in your life and love, to *overcome* my old nature's fleshly instincts, and to *welcome* your Spirit's present over-flowing of my being!"

There *is* an answer to that prayer.

To assist and enable our living as *conduits,* or conductors, of Christ's life and power, heaven has designed a remarkably beautiful plan: *Gift-giving.* Why? Because just as we could never *save* ourselves without the gift of salvation (see Rom. 6:23), and just as we could never *live* for Christ without the gift of the Holy Spirit's indwelling (see Acts 2:37–38), similarly, we can never *give* the gospel in the fullness of Christ's power without the spiritual gifts the Holy Spirit affords us.

Spiritual gifts are heaven's "delivery systems." They make possible the entry of God's "kingdom graces" here and now, just as Jesus said the Holy Spirit would. He said the Comforter/Helper—the Holy Spirit—would manifest Christ's own life and power through believers by transmitting "things" God wants to do through us just as He did "things" through His Son.

> He will glorify Me, for He will take of what is Mine and declare it to you. All things that the Father has are Mine. Therefore I said that He will take of Mine and declare it to you. (John 16:14–15)

How the Holy Spirit distributes gifts and the way He works in each of us is often widely varied. Each believer is used in distinct ways. To help us understand this variety of operations and manifestations of the Spirit, the Bible provides a vivid picture. Each believer in Christ is shown as being joined into one body, as a member, or "body part," if you will. We need to treasure and apply the truth this picture reveals, for two reasons:

1. We need to understand how true it is that, during this era *only* by the Holy Spirit's power in and through the church, the living Christ can relate to and release His will and working in the world.

> And He [God the Father] put all things under His [God the Son's] feet, and gave Him to be head over all things to the church, which is His body, the fullness of Him [God the Holy Spirit] who fills all in all. (Eph. 1:22–23)

2. We need to appreciate how true it is that every one of us has a different role, just as a body has different members that function in different ways.

> For as we have many members in one body, but all the members do not have the same function, so we, being many, are one body in Christ, and individually members of one another. (Rom. 12:4–5)

A full study of the gifts of the Holy Spirit isn't possible in this book, but we must grasp two things: First, it is essential that each of us be *informed* and *desirous* of spiritual gifts:

> Now concerning spiritual gifts, brethren, I do not want you to be ignorant. (1 Cor. 12:1)

> Pursue love, and desire spiritual gifts. (1 Cor. 14:1)

Second, it is essential that each of us is open to the gifts the Holy Spirit wants to work in us. Becoming informed of the possibilities isn't difficult, and the pathway expressing our availability is scripturally clear. Such passages of Scripture as Romans 12:3–21 and 1 Corinthians 12:1–31 are replete with listings of spiritual gifts. They also discuss the mood, manner, and attitude that open most readily to the Holy Spirit's gifts and the atmosphere in which those gifts are best received and exercised. But foremost in our analysis, we'll find that the most important trait to allow the Holy Spirit to cultivate in us is *love*.

When the Holy Spirit is welcomed to work freely in our lives, the supernatural fullness of the love He outpours can remove hindering resistance and make us spiritual superconductors; that is, men and women through whom the life, traits, and power of Jesus Himself are revealed *today!*

Supernaturally begotten love will:

- *fire our passions* with a desire to worship and glorify Jesus Christ, and witness to His goodness;

- *beget a constant desire* to walk steadfastly in the Spirit, faithful to the truth;

- *sustain an abiding hunger and thirst* for righteousness, which assures abiding fullness;
- *animate our pursuit* of and employment of the gifts He gives, and edify and enlarge Christ's body;

- *maintain a servant-like heart* toward mankind, keeping us available to serve human need; and

- *assure our readiness* as conduits of divine power through whom supernatural graces flow.

And with all the above, true Holy Spirit-begotten love will:

- *deter us* from sectarian smallness, racial insensitivity, doctrinaire divisiveness, or judgmental criticism *and join us* all as one body in Christ, filled and overflowing with the glory of Jesus through His church!

* * *

"Boy, Pastor sure hit a home run tonight, didn't he?"

Kendra's enthusiasm was shared. Tom and Julie expressed their strong agreement, responding immediately to their daughter's assessment of the message they had just heard at church.

"It's interesting, isn't it?" Tom asked, not directing his question to anyone specifically. The boys—Kent and Laney—had just come in, having finished their assigned chore of wheeling the garbage containers to the curb since the refuse collector came early on Monday mornings.

"What's interesting, Dad?" Kent inquired.

"I was thinking about what Kendra said when we came in."

"What's that, sis?"

"Oh, I was only commenting on what a great teaching that was tonight. It made me so happy to see the way Pastor put both the love and the power of the Holy Spirit side by side. You know, he didn't back down on the promises of what the Lord can do today, but he didn't turn supernatural living into a power trip."

"That's pretty level-headed thinking, young lady." Her mother was donning an apron, knowing her clan would be ready for a pre-bedtime, Sunday-night snack. "I agree, but I don't know if I could have put it any better, if as well."

"Well, that's what I meant by interesting," Dad interjected. "Here, without making any push for being spiritual today, we seem to have been talking about the Holy Spirit for hours—and especially about how beautiful His workings can be if they're kept uncluttered by our fears or selfish confusion."

Kendra added, "Dad, that's exactly what I prayed for—you know, when Pastor invited us all to a *season* of prayer near the end of the service? I prayed, 'Lord, fill Your whole church with power today—and start right here with me.'" Tom went over and gave his high-school girl a warm hug, saying, "Terrific, Honey. It sounds like a prayer for all of us to learn and live . . . ," and as he looked at his wife she winked. "*Today.*"

Tom and Julie both felt a surge of gratitude for their daughter's insight—and for their family. By now, Kent had crowded beside his mom at the refrigerator on a search for snackable items. Tom and Kendra were sliding up to the table.

And Laney was running down the hall toward his room—motor roaring again, at thirty-five thousand feet.

Personal Evaluation

We covered a lot of ground in this chapter concerning the Holy Spirit. Some of the key points of the chapter have been repeated below. Circle the answer that best represents your level of agreement:

I believe the following about the Holy Spirit:

1. He is God.
   Disagree   Somewhat disagree   Somewhat agree   Agree

2. He inspired the Scriptures.
   Disagree   Somewhat disagree   Somewhat agree   Agree

3. He is the inseminator of the Incarnation.
   Disagree   Somewhat disagree   Somewhat agree   Agree

4. He instructs mankind.
   Disagree   Somewhat disagree   Somewhat agree   Agree

5. He gives us new life.
   Disagree   Somewhat disagree   Somewhat agree   Agree

6. He gives us all gifts.
   Disagree   Somewhat disagree   Somewhat agree   Agree

7. He wants to fill us.
   Disagree   Somewhat disagree   Somewhat agree   Agree

In the Group

1. Is it difficult for you to think of the Holy Spirit as a *person?* Many of us have been guilty of referring to Him as *it.* Why do you think that is? What was it that made the Holy Spirit more personal to you?

2. When you think of the Holy Spirit's work in the past, what sort of things come to your mind? By that question, I'm asking you to reflect on the Holy Spirit's work at creation, in Old Testament times, at the time of Christ, in the early stages of the church, etc.

3. How do you experience the fruit of the Spirit in your own personal life? How would you explain to someone else the process involved in practically relating to love, joy, peace, and the like?

4. What does it mean to be "filled with the Spirit?" Perhaps you can discuss not only what it means but what it doesn't mean. Why do you think this is a subject with so much debate? How can you contribute to the unity of the body within the context of this issue?

5. What is your spiritual gift or gifts? How did you discover your gift? Is there a difference between a gift and a talent or ability? Explain your answer. Have your beliefs regarding the Holy Spirit changed since you were a young Christian, or have they stayed relatively the same?

6. Spend some time in prayer with your partner. Update him on the requests he's been praying for, and have him do the same with you. Raise any new requests you may have and conclude the time with a conversation with your heavenly Father.

Memory Verse: "When the Counselor comes, whom I will send to you from the Father, the Spirit of truth who goes out from the Father, he will testify about me" (John 15:26 NIV).

Chapter Eight

The Redemption of Man

by Dr. Rod Cooper

I WAS HOT, tired, sweaty, discouraged, and most of all—*angry!* I had what my friends affectionately call a "stupid attack."

Let me explain. I had just finished playing a round of golf. It was one of those rounds where you leave the course knowing that the only thing about your game that has improved is your prayer life. After stuffing my golf bag in the trunk of the car and changing shoes, I was ready to go home. I was sitting in my two-seater sports car, a Honda CRX, which means there is not a lot of room.

I have a pouch where I keep my valuables like my money, car keys, and wedding ring. I was emptying my pouch into my hand when it happened. My hands were a little sweaty from the round of golf. Instead of taking my time to wipe them off with my towel, I proceeded to put on my wedding ring. As fate would have it, the ring slipped out of my sweaty hands and dropped through a narrow opening next to the emergency brake. The emergency brake is down by the driver's right hand. I looked through the crack and could see the ring precariously hanging on to a little bolt.

I tried to reach for it with a little pen knife I had, but it was just out of reach. My frustration was mounting. I was already late for dinner, so I made a decision. This is where the "stupid attack" happened. I thought if I drove home slowly enough, the ring would stay stationary, and I could get the proper tools from my garage to extricate it.

I began my journey home, stopping every few feet to make sure the ring was still there. After about the fourth stop, I looked—and guess what—yep, no ring. I got out of my car, slid under it and looked, but no ring. I retraced my steps for the several hundred feet I had gone— no ring. I got down on my hands and knees and crawled over the several hundred feet as if I were looking for a contact lens—no ring. I drove home discouraged and angry at myself, repeatedly reminding myself that I could have called my wife and told her what tool to bring me. But noooo!

It was dinnertime when I got home, but I refused to eat. Instead I stormed into the garage and tore apart the emergency-brake assembly, hoping against hope I would find it. Alas, no ring. I was depressed for weeks.

Why the mad search for *this* ring? It was only, at most, a fifty-dollar gold band. It was because of what it *represented*. It had tremendous value to me. You see, it was my father-in-law's wedding band. He could not wear it because of an accident that had caused his finger to swell up; the doctor had been forced to cut the ring off. There was not enough gold in the ring, after cutting it off, for the ring to fit his finger. After my father-in-law and his wife talked, they offered the ring to me. They wanted me to wear it as a continual reminder of their love and support of our marriage. Every time I put it on, it reminded me not only of the bond between my wife and me, but also of her family's commitment and love for us . . . for me.

That ring was special—it was valuable, one of a kind. In one final desperate attempt, I took the Honda to a garage and asked them to tear the car apart to find the ring. They kept it for the whole day but could not find it. I felt a tremendous loss. I would have done almost anything to have gotten the ring back.

Maybe something similar has happened to you. You know the disappointment and ache that comes from losing something that is precious and valuable to you. You know what it is like to search for it and long for its return. So does God.

God was like Hallmark greeting cards: He cared enough to send the very best. Throughout the pages of Scripture, we see the Lord longing, pursuing, and ultimately sacrificing Himself for our return. Have you ever wondered why? Why this relentless pursuit by God for our return? What is so valuable about us that God would send His only son? Why would Jesus endure such cruelty and brutality from those He was there to rescue? As the psalmist declared, "What is man that thou art mindful of him?" (Ps. 8:4 KJV). Apparently God sees something in us that we too often fail to see in each other. What could that be?

In His Image

We live in a culture with a distorted value system. It's like the story Tony Campolo tells in his book, *Who Switched the Price Tags?* He says when he was a boy he and a friend dreamed of slipping into a store and changing all the price tags. Suddenly trivial items would be expensive and valuable merchandise would cost next to nothing.

That's what seems to have happened in our society today. What used to be valuable is no longer sacred. Case in point: This past week I read about a father who confessed to the brutal beating and death of his three-year-old son. The reason? "He would not come when I told him to," the father explained.

Why are people so angry today? Why are we so quick to react rather than reflect? Why are we so interested in feeling happy rather than in being holy? Could it be that we have bought into a system that has switched the price tags on what makes us valuable? I believe so.

I believe some evidence of the price tags being switched is how we originally came to be here. There are those who believe in evolution. They say that millions of years ago lifeless matter, acted upon by natural forces, gave origin to one or more minute living organisms that have since evolved into all living and extinct plants and animals, including mankind. Other evolutionists would add to that by saying that mankind is a direct descendant of apes and monkeys.

Doesn't that make you feel good about yourself? Next time you go to the zoo you could be looking at Aunt Jane behind the bars. Just thinking about this possibility makes me feel warm all over—I mean an angry warm.

The point is this: If we are cosmic accidents, then we have no destiny. Therefore mankind is no more valuable than a tree or a rock or a dog. R. C. Sproul put it well when he said, "If we emerge from the slime by accident and finally disintegrate into a void or abyss of nothingness, then we live our lives between two poles of absolute meaninglessness. We are peeled zeroes, stripped naked of dignity and worth."[1] The only way to live, then, is to reach for all of the gusto *now* because this is it. There are no absolutes. There is no future, and thus there is no hope. Life becomes a search for thrills, living for the weekend and working frantically to get a bigger paycheck and a larger house.

Our value is then based upon who we know, what we do, or what we own. It becomes true that the one who has the most toys when he dies wins. If mankind has no destiny then he has no value. The price tags have been swapped; in the beginning it was not this way.

I have some good news for our bad times. God sent His only Son, Jesus, to die on a cross to redeem us because He has a future and a hope for us. Jesus came to switch the price tags back. Our origin and our destiny are tied to God. In God's book we are heading somewhere. We are the bride of Christ. We are going to reign with Him. We are the cosmic Cinderellas upon which God has placed the glass slipper of salvation. You see, to be created by God is to be related to God. But what makes us so special to God that He has a plan for us? Read the following words:

> God said, "Let us make man in *Our image,* according to *Our likeness*: let them have dominion over the fish of the sea, over the birds of the air, and over the cattle, over all of the earth and over every creeping thing that creeps on the earth." So God created man in *His own image*; in the *image of God* He created him; male and female, He created them." (Gen. 1:26–27 NKJV, emphasis mine)

Did you see it? We were made in the *image of God.* We are little reflections of our Creator. We were made with the unique capacity to mirror and reflect the character of God. But what is God's *image?* The scope of God's image is not completely spelled out anywhere in Scripture, but Genesis 1:1–25 seems to give us some solid ideas.

For instance, the context of creation as set forth in this passage shows God to be personal, rational, having intelligence and will, and able to form plans and execute them. The passage seems to show God as being creative, emotional, competent to control the world He has made, and morally perfect in that all He created was good.

Even though God transcends us in power, glory, and His being, we mirror Him in many ways. We, as human beings, are also creative and intelligent and emotional. We are moral agents equipped with a mind and heart and will and the ability to make decisions and carry them out. We also are personal and social beings who desire to be in relationship. These elements make it possible for us to *represent* God's moral character, to *rule* or have responsible dominion over creation, and to be in *relationship* with God and one another.

Yet there is a problem. All of the elements that make up the image of God in people (both men and women) seem to be internal, or what theologians would call "immaterial." But what about our bodies? God doesn't have a body and yet seems to take great pains in pointing out how He created us as both spirit and flesh.

The Bible is clear in that God created us as a unity—of body and soul. Charles Ryrie put it well when he said, "Man's body is included in the Image of God. While God is not physical in any way, there is a sense in which even a man's body is included in the image of God. His body is a fit instrument for the self-expression of the soul made for fellowship with the creator and is suited in the future to become a spiritual body (1 Cor. 15:44)."[2] The body is important to the Lord in that He "became flesh and dwelt among us" (John 1:14 NKJV), and after the resurrection, He came back in a body and will have it for eternity. The body itself is a miracle of God. Think about it. A person can have up to five million hairs (I think I only have about five hundred—and that is pushing it). The body has 20 square feet of skin; 650 muscles; 9,000 taste buds on the tongue; 107,000,000 cells in each eye; 206 bones; 60,000 miles of arteries, veins, and capillaries; and 13 billion nerve cells—and that is just the beginning. No wonder the psalmist declared that we are "fearfully and wonderfully made" (Ps. 139:14 NKJV).

The biblical view of the body is that it is created good and has no inherent evil in its physical makeup. Yet it suffers from moral corruption just like the soul. Mankind is sinful in both body and soul.

Christianity teaches not redemption from the body but redemption *of* the body.

Max Lucado is one of my favorite writers. He has a wonderful way of painting verbal pictures. Experience his words as he describes how it might have been on the day man was created in God's image.

> He placed one scoop of clay upon another until a form lay lifeless on the ground. All of the garden's inhabitants paused to witness the event. Hawks hovered. Giraffes stretched. Trees bowed. Butterflies paused on petals and watched. "You will love me, nature," God said. "I have made you that way. You will obey me, universe. For you were designed to do so. You will reflect my glory, skies, for that is how you were created. But this one will be like me. This one will be able to choose." Creation stood in silence and gazed upon the lifeless form. . . . The maker looked earnestly at the clay creation. A monsoon of love swelled up within him . . . God's form bent over the sculptured face and breathed. Dust stirred on the lips of the new one. The chest rose, cracking the red mud. The cheeks fleshened. A finger moved. And an eye opened. But more incredible than the moving of the flesh was the stirring of the spirit. Those who could see the unseen gasped. Perhaps it was the wind who said it first. Perhaps what the star saw that moment is what made it blink ever since. Maybe it was left to an angel to whisper it: "It looks like . . . it appears so much like . . . it is him!" "It's eternal," gasped another. Within the man, God had placed a divine seed. A seed of his self. . . . The Creator had created not a creature, but another creator.[3]

This makes me feel special. This makes me feel warm all over—the *good* kind of warm. It gives me purpose and meaning. Most of all, this knowledge of the image of God changes the way I respond to my friends, to my family, and even to strangers. If God respects and values them, then so do I. As James points out in chapter 3 of his epistle, we must not curse our fellow human being on the ground that he was made in the image of God (v. 9).

So what happened? How did we get from the penthouse to the outhouse? When did the price tags change? Remember—part of the image of God is that ability to choose, and a choice was made in the beginning that totally changed the price tags.

Humpty Dumpty Had a Great Fall

A favorite nursery rhyme is the familiar story of an egg that takes an unfortunate tumble:

> Humpty Dumpty sat on a wall;
> Humpty Dumpty had a great fall.
> All the king's horses and all the king's men
> Couldn't put Humpty together again.

According to those who know about such things, this piece of wisdom is a relic that is thousands of years old. Versions have appeared in eight European languages. In its primitive stages, however, Humpty Dumpty was a riddle. It asked the question: What, when broken, can never be repaired, not even by strong or wise individuals? As any child knows, the answer is an egg. Regardless of how hard we try, a broken egg can never be put back together again. We simply have to learn to live with the mess.

There is a Humpty Dumpty story in the Bible. We call it the Fall. Adam and Eve eat the forbidden fruit. They claim they possess the necessary wisdom to be like God. But when the dust settles, Adam and Eve are not perched on a lofty plain. They have fallen. Regardless of how hard we try, things can never be put back together again.

Our contemporary fall is seen in the feeling that things just do not work anymore. Our lives appear out of control. Changes take place faster than we can cope. Broken eggs are an appropriate symbol. Wherever we step, we hear the crunch of fragile shells beneath our feet.

Genesis 3 gives the account of undoubtedly the most tragic event in the history of the world. It appears that the sin of Satan and his cohorts had already taken place before our first parents were tempted and sinned. You see, Satan was the one who made it possible to change the price tags. He sneaked into the store. Like a spurned lover who could not have his or her way, Satan's vendetta was to take away from God that which was most precious to Him, namely mankind. Originally, mankind was to rule the earth with God as vice regent.

Psalm 8 declares:

> What is man that Thou dost take thought of him?
> And the son of man, that Thou dost care for him?
> Yet Thou hast made him a little lower than God,
> And dost crown him with glory and majesty!
> Thou dost make him to rule over the works of Thy hands;
> Thou hast put all things under his feet. (vv. 4–6)

Not even the highest cherub, Satan, could say he was made in God's image. Satan's attitude was like that of a spoiled child who said, "If I can't have it, then neither can you." Satan apparently used a creature with which Adam and Eve were familiar to carry out his plans (see Gen. 3:1). Satan's scheme was to create doubt in Eve's mind concerning the goodness of God in placing one restriction upon the couple, namely not eating from the tree of knowledge (see Gen. 3:1–3).

Even today, most of our problems come when we begin to doubt the goodness of God. Satan denied what God said was true—literally calling God a liar. Then Satan challenged Eve to act independently of God and thus become like Him. She had a choice—no, *they* had a choice. She chose and ate, and then offered some to Adam, who chose and ate as well.

Thus the Fall. Their act of sin led to separation, or estrangement, from God. They were driven out of the garden. Satan offered them an illusion. He essentially said, "You can have paradise and more." Sound familiar? We hear the same song but a different verse today: "You can have it all. If you can just make it to that next level, you can have it all."

Consequences of the Fall

Ever since the garden experience, mankind has been struggling to make its own way. A church historian says, "The loss of paradise is the Bible's way of describing 'original sin.' It is the condition in which all people find themselves, separated from God yet longing for the inner contentment they once knew in his presence. We are like marionettes that have cut their own strings in the hope of finding another way to dance, but find out too late that without the strings they cannot dance at all."[4] When mankind fell, it fell hard. What were the devastating consequences of our first parents' choice?

"For All Have Sinned . . ."

Just as a climber on a mountaintop can dislodge a pebble that rolls and accumulates others until it launches an avalanche that can move the whole side of a mountain, so Adam's sin in the Garden of Eden dislodged a pebble that has built into an avalanche of sin and death sweeping through our entire race.

Adam's sin was the "original" sin. It can never be repeated. Romans 5:12 says, "You know the story of how Adam landed us in the dilemma we're in—first sin, then death, and no one exempt from either sin or death" (TM). Adam and Eve became sinners. Adam and Eve sinned, but all of us since then, except Christ, sin because we are sinners.

Adam and Eve got a sin nature because they sinned, but we sin because we have a sin nature. We are sinners in Adam. We are born into a state of sinfulness. We are seen by God as sinful because of our solidarity with Adam. This does not seem fair. "Why am I being punished for something over which I had no choice or control?" This is a question often asked about the consequences of Adam's sin for the whole human race.

Watchmen Nee, a famous theologian, once remarked, "We have all sinned in Adam."

"I don't understand," one man cried out.

Nee replied, "If your great-grandfather had died at the age of three, where would you be? You would have died in him! Your experience is bound up in his. And in just the same way your experience is bound up with that of Adam's." So we are all involved in Adam's sin because we are born in Adam.

King David put it well when he said, "I was sinful at birth, sinful from the time my mother conceived me" (Ps. 51:5). One of the key consequences of the Fall was the entrance of sin into the world and into us. Sin may be defined as lack of conformity to the law of God in act, habit, attitude, outlook, disposition, and motivation. Sin has been referred to as missing the mark, like the archer shooting and missing the bull's-eye.

Oftentimes when we think of *sin,* we are really thinking of *sins.* Sins are personal acts against God's standards. We will oftentimes say "so and so has sinned," thinking of such things as stealing or lying. But behind the actions is the attitude. Being a sinner means that at the very core of our being we have a sin nature that is a desire and propensity to take care of ourselves first and foremost without depending upon God. We are utterly self-centered.

R. C. Sproul talks about the central motivation of sin in our lives by saying, "Even the smallest sin is an act of rebellion against God. Every sin is an act of cosmic treason, a futile attempt to dethrone God in his sovereign authority."[5]

As a result of the first sin, a fallen nature is passed on from parent to child. After Adam and Eve sinned the first time, it became natural for them to disbelieve and disobey God. They passed on to their children a sin nature, and their children passed it on to theirs, and the process continues. "For all have sinned and come short of the glory of God" (Rom. 2:23 NKJV). Sin is both personal and social, individual and collective. It is sin that has estranged us from God.

Total Depravity

Mark Twain accurately summed up mankind's condition when he said, "Man was created a little lower than the angels, and he has been getting a little lower ever since." Nowhere was this more obvious than in the newspaper story that reported that a gunman had opened fire on a police officer during a chase, and while the officer lay bleeding on the ground with five bullets in his body, a crowd tried to rob him.

The Bible teaches the total depravity of the human race. The concept of total depravity does not mean that depraved people cannot or do not do things that are good in either man's or God's sight. It just means that those actions can in no way gain favor with God for salvation. Nor does the concept of total depravity mean that fallen man has no conscience or moral center that helps him discern between good and evil. But his conscience has been affected by the Fall and therefore cannot be a safe and reliable guide. Finally, it does not mean that people indulge in every form of sin or in any sin to the greatest extent possible. This would be utter depravity, i.e., to be as wicked as one could possibly be.

You and I sin, but we could sin more severely than we actually do. Aleksandr Solzhenitsyn said, "If only there were evil people somewhere insidiously committing evil deeds, and it were necessary only to separate them from the rest of us and destroy them. But the line dividing good and evil cuts through the heart of every human being. And who is willing to destroy a piece of his own heart?"

Total depravity means that the corruption of the Fall has extended to every part of our being. Our minds, our wills, and our bodies are affected by evil. We speak sinful words, have ungodly thoughts, and do sinful deeds.

Total depravity also means that because of that corruption, there is nothing man can do to merit saving favor with God. We are unable to save ourselves apart from the grace of God. Because of our depraved condition, Scripture says we are "dead in trespasses and sins" (Eph. 2:1 NKJV). We are "sold under sin" (Rom. 7:14 NKJV), and we are "by nature children of wrath" (Eph. 2:3 NKJV).

Yet it amazes me how unaware people are of their lostness until it's too late. In his essays George Orwell offered a graphic image of human lostness. Orwell described a wasp that "was sucking jam on my plate, and I cut him in half. He paid no attention, merely went on with his meal, while a tiny stream of jam trickled out of his severed esophagus. Only when he tried to fly away did he grasp the dreadful thing that had happened to him."

Orwell's wasp and people without Christ have much in common. Severed from their souls, but greedy and unaware, people continue to consume life's sweetness. Only when it's time to fly away will they grasp their dreadful condition. Only by the quickening power of the Holy Spirit may we be brought out of this terrible state.

The Grim Reaper

Another key consequence of the Fall is death.

In our society we do everything we can to cover up the fact that one of these days we are going to die. I went to a funeral recently, and as I listened to people talk about the deceased, they would say such things as "he passed away" or "he is no longer with us." Rarely did I hear anyone say the person was dead.

Today, some people's fear of death is so strong and their confidence in technology is so great that they are spending tens of thousands of dollars to have their bodies frozen at the time of death. They hope they might be revived to live again when a cure is found for whatever caused their death. The fact that a man knows he will die colors all of his life and sets him apart from the rest of God's creatures.

I have just turned forty years of age. I am a counselor, and therefore, I know all of the implications of turning forty. More of my life has passed than what may be left. I thought knowing all of the implications of turning forty and counseling other men as they went through their midlife crises would spare me my own midlife crisis (I prefer to call it a *transition*). It didn't.

When I turned forty, I began to wake up at night with cold sweats, thinking about death. It really hit me that I was mortal and couldn't do anything about it. For the first time in my life, I realized I had very little control, and the best I could do in life was manage. We all know that death is not natural; God did not intend for us to have to die. Yet when our original parents sinned, death entered the world.

In fact, there are three forms of death in the world as a result of Adam and Eve's sin. There is spiritual death, or separation from God. There is physical death. Finally, there is the possibility of eternal death if one does not trust God's gracious provision for us through Christ Jesus. Hell is eternal separation from God: no second chances.

Yet, even though death is the end, it is not final. The Scripture is clear that, "As it is appointed unto men *once* to die, but after this, the judgment" (Heb. 9:27 KJV, emphasis mine). We all have a future and a destiny. What we decide now will determine that future's pain or pleasure.

Putting the Pieces Back Together Again

There is a wonderful new technology today called Direct TV. If you have a spare eight hundred dollars, you can buy an eighteen-inch satellite dish and have direct access to more than 150 channels. Without needing a cable box to unscramble the signal, you can, through the use of your satellite dish, connect directly to channels for movies, sporting events, and numerous other programs that may interest you. You might say that our original parents, Adam and Eve, were like Direct TV. They did not need a mediator; they could have direct access to God. They talked to Him daily in the garden and had unbroken fellowship. They could enjoy directly the fullness of having a relationship with their Creator. When the Fall took place, that direct access was gone.

Since that time, you might say we all are born "cable-ready." In my house, our TV is hooked up to cable service. With my subscription, I get what is called the basic package. I have access to a number of local channels as well as to a few special channels, like ESPN. Yet my TV is not operating to its fullest capability because there are a number of channels I cannot get.

We also have what I call basic cable when we are born. We can enjoy God's general revelation. We can smile at a child's playfulness, stand in awe at the power of the oceans, and feel emotional ecstasy at a beautiful symphony. But we cannot appreciate all life has to offer or live it to its fullest because much of life is scrambled, like the TV channels, and does not make sense. We need a cable box to fully enjoy all that is offered in this life and to utilize our fullest potential. The "cable box," of course, is Jesus Christ. It is only through Him that we are able to see life and live life as God intended. Only through Jesus can life be unscrambled. Only through Jesus can "Humpty Dumpty" be put back on the wall.

In the Fall of mankind, severe consequences took place. The Fall, however, did not destroy our humanity. Though our ability to reflect God's holiness is lost, we are still human. We still have a heart, a mind, and a will. We still bear the stamp of our Creator. And from God's standpoint, we still have a future, a hope, and a destiny to fulfill. The Lord planned for our salvation from the beginning.

Starting Over

Because of the Fall, men and women face two critical needs in their lives. First, they need to be restored to fellowship with God so they might fulfill all that God has intended for them. We are sinners, and we stand guilty before God, desperately in need of forgiveness.

The Bible is explicit about our condition without a personal relationship with Christ. We are lost (Luke 19:10), condemned (John 3:18), under God's wrath (John 3:36), dead in trespasses and sin (Eph. 2:1), having no hope and without God in the world (Eph. 2:12), and unrighteous (Rom. 1:19–32). The religious and nonreligious, the educated and uneducated, the rich and the poor are all in need of God's intervention and are hopelessly lost without it. If mankind is to experience salvation, God Himself must do the work.

This leads me to the second point. We are spiritually impotent. We do not have the power or the resources necessary to restore ourselves to fellowship with God. I liken mankind's condition to that of a patient going to the dentist. Usually before going to the dentist, we brush our teeth super-thoroughly to ensure their spotlessness under examination. But when we're there, the dentist can swish a red liquid around our mouth that reveals (to our dismay) a tremendous amount of plaque and other material we could not remove with all our brushing. The dentist alone has the equipment to adequately remove it.

Likewise, we may try on our own to be clean before God and even do a good job of convincing ourselves. But God's Spirit has a way of exposing our true sinfulness and our need for a divine "dentist" to make us clean. In short, men and women need something done *for* them and something done *in* them.

But the question is *what?* We are sinners, and therefore we sin. We also know that all sin is an offense to God; therefore we are offensive to God. God is the norm, the standard, the criterion of judging right from wrong. Sin is an offense against Him and His holy character. So how can God remain holy and just and at the same time forgive the sinner and allow him or her into His presence? God cannot tolerate sin or behold evil. So how can mankind ever be restored to Him?

The Substitute

A substitute is someone who takes the place of or acts instead of another. For instance, during a war between Britain and France, men were drafted into the French army by a kind of lottery system. When someone's name was drawn, he had to go off to battle.

There was one exception to this, however. A person could be exempt if another man was willing to take his place. On one occasion, the authorities came to a certain man and told him he was among those who had been chosen. He refused to go, saying, "I was shot two years ago."

At first they questioned his sanity, but he insisted that was indeed the case. He claimed that the military records would show that he had been killed in action.

"How can that be?" they questioned. "You are alive now!"

He explained that when his name had come up, a close friend said to him, "You have a large family, but I am not married and no one is dependent on me. I will take your name and address and go in your place." And that is indeed what the record showed.

This rather unusual case was referred to Napoleon Bonaparte, who decided that the country had no legal claim on that man. He was free. He had died in the person of another. A substitute had died in his place.

We also are in need of a substitute. We need someone who can pay our debt—and that debt is death (see Rom. 6:23)—and clean us out so that we can be found blameless according to the Lord's morally perfect standard.

Our substitute would have to be uninfected by the disease of depravity—totally sinless. He would have to measure up to God's standards in every way while still remaining human so he could take our place. He would have to be deity as well as a morally perfect man both by nature and by choice. He would have to be—God's Son—Jesus.

The Provision

God is the only one who could solve the problem man's sin presented. So even before the Fall happened, God's plan was at work on our restoration to Himself.

God's plan of redemption has always been present throughout Scripture. From the time God clothed Adam and Eve with the skins of slain animals, the great program of redemption through blood was begun. In Genesis 3:15, we see the promise that mankind would be redeemed by the Savior when we read that the seed of the woman would inflict a fatal wound upon Satan. The Savior, of course, would be Jesus Christ. The sacrifices of the Old Testament were symbols of Him, the One who was to come—God in human flesh—to be our substitute. The animal sacrifices of the Old Testament were only temporary, but Jesus' sacrifice of Himself was "for all time" (Heb. 10:12a).

God has provided a way for us to be "justified freely by his grace through the redemption that came by Christ Jesus" (Rom. 3:24). The Lord has done this by giving His only begotten Son as a sacrifice for us.

Salvation means to be rescued from some calamity. However, the Bible also uses the term *salvation* in a specific sense to refer to our ultimate redemption from sin and reconciliation to God. Our salvation through Christ, then, is our rescue from the ultimate calamity—the judgment of God. God has done this by presenting Jesus "as a sacrifice of atonement, through faith in his blood. He did this to demonstrate his justice, because in his forbearance he had left the sins committed beforehand unpunished—he did it to demonstrate his justice at the present time, so as to be just and the one who justifies those who have faith in Jesus" (Rom. 3:25–26). The key word in these verses is *justified*. Even though we are still sinful, we are declared righteous by God , because of what Jesus has done.

Charles Swindoll gives an excellent illustration of the concept of justification. He says,

> Imagine a courtroom scene with God as the judge and us as the accused. The Lord looks down on us and asks, "Have you loved me with all your being?" Ashamed, we look up at Him and answer, "No, your honor." Next, He asks, "Have you loved others as you have loved yourself?" Again we answer in the negative. Finally, He asks, "Do you believe you are sinners, and do you trust in my son's payment for your sin?" "Yes, your honor." Then we hear the words of amazing grace falling from God's lips:

"Since My Son, Jesus Christ, has paid for your debt and you have accepted his payment, you are hereby fully pardoned."[6]

Notice that in no way have we gotten our salvation the old-fashioned way—by earning it. We receive our salvation through the work of Christ alone. He has done the work; all we must do is receive. Ephesians 2:8–9 puts it well: "For by grace are ye saved through faith; and that not of yourselves: it is the gift of God: not of works, lest any man should boast" (KJV). All it takes to change the price tags back to where they belong is to trust or have believing faith in what Jesus has done. Believing faith is like the man who was climbing a narrow path up a mountain and lost his footing. He was plummeting down the mountainside to his death when out of desperation he reached out to grab a tree sticking out of the side of the mountain. For the moment he was safe; then he heard the tree limb beginning to break. Out of desperation he cried out and said, "God, if You are up there, would You please save me?"

To his surprise a voice answered back saying, "I am here, My son."

The man once again cried out and said, "Please rescue me from here."

The heavenly voice replied, "Then let go, and I will save you."

The man thought about it for a while and said, "Hey, is there anybody else up there?"

This man did not have believing faith. Believing faith is letting go and trusting only in the provision God has made through His Son Jesus Christ.

Salvation Is Not Ancient History but Current Events

There is a story of an illiterate couple who had just recently trusted Christ. They met with a group of believers who dressed alike. The men wore red shirts while engaged in a certain project, so the woman made one for her husband. He came home from the meeting with a look of disappointment on his face because others had a message printed on their shirts, but he did not.

His wife, undaunted by her inability to read, sewed three words on his shirt that she copied from a sign in a store window across the street.

He wore it to the next meeting and came home bubbling with joy. He said all of the men really liked the inscription because it so aptly described the wonderful change they had seen in his life.

It turned out his wife had written UNDER NEW MANAGEMENT.

We were the slaves of sin and Satan, but now we are ruled by God and His truth. We have truly been freed from a cruel taskmaster and have come under the direction of One who gives freedom and everlasting life. What are some of the benefits of being under new management?

I'm So Glad I'm a Part of the Family of God

"Therefore if any man be in Christ, he is a new creature: old things are passed away; behold, all things are become new" (2 Cor. 5:17 KJV). There is an old saying in the African-American church that says, "The day I was saved, my feet got a brand new walk and my speech got a brand new talk."

Why? Because now I am a child of God. The Bible declares that I have been adopted into the family (Rom. 8:15). Adoption in the Bible means to be placed as an adult son in God's family with all of the rights, privileges, and responsibilities of sonship. Our citizenship is in heaven (see Eph. 2:19). We are fellow citizens with other saints in God's kingdom.

Forgiven

Trusting Christ erases our sins. The penalty incurred by sin is erased, but not because God has become lenient. God's forgiveness is not based upon His feeling sorry for us but on the shed blood of Christ. When we trust Christ as Savior, our sins no longer condemn us because Christ bore the penalty for us. We confess our sins, but this is so we might enjoy fellowship with God and have a solid walk with God. All of our sins—past, present, and future—are covered by the blood of Christ. Never again will they condemn us. This is all a part of God's forgiveness of sins. We can truly say, "Free at last, free at last. Thank God Almighty I am free at last."

Members of a Royal Priesthood

We are called "a kingdom and priests" (Rev. 1:6). This priesthood is said to be holy (see 1 Pet. 2:5). The work of a priest involves sacrifice. We are called upon to be "living sacrifices" (Rom. 12:1) for God. The praise of our lips and the good works we do are sacrifices that are well-pleasing to God (Heb. 13:15–16). As believer priests, we have direct access through Christ to God and have the assurance of a future reign with Christ (see Rev. 5:10).

No Wasted Experience

God is using every event in our lives to make us look like His Son—Jesus. Romans 8:28 says, "And we know that all things work together for good to them that love God, to them that are called according to his purpose" (KJV). The key word here is *good*, which in this context means that which fits us for heaven and conforms us to the image of Christ. Every day God is using the experience in your life to conform you to the image of His Son.

There is a story about a young man and an elderly man working together in a gold-processing plant. The young man told the old man he wanted to try to determine when the gold was ready. The old man said, "Come and get me when you think the gold is ready."

After a couple of hours the young man said, "I think the gold is ready."

The old man said, "Nope—not ready."

After four hours the young man said, "It's ready."

The old man said, "Nope—not ready."

After six hours the young man said, "It has to be ready now."

The old man said, "Come with me."

They arrived at the pot of gold with the flames licking underneath. The old man said to the young man, "Do you see all of that dirt coming off of the gold? We call that *dross*. We do not want that in the gold. You will know that the gold is ready when you can look into the pot of gold and see only the reflection of your face."

Similarly, every day God is helping us to get rid of the dross in our lives. This is the sanctification process. Every day God is helping us, through trials, to set more and more of our lives apart unto Him. He is doing this so when people look at us, they will see only the reflection of His face in all that we do. Hopefully, like the disciples of old, our lifestyle will be so different that the world will have to say, "Surely these men have been with Jesus" (see Acts 4:13).

Conclusion

By God's grace the price tags have been switched back. Humpty Dumpty can be put together again. We now can become all that God has intended for us to become because of what He has done for us and in us.

If you were to come to our home in Castle Rock, Colorado, you would be treated to a fabulous gourmet meal and a dog show. Nancy is an excellent gourmet chef and tickles our guests' taste buds with her wonderful culinary delights. She also is an excellent dog trainer. We have two miniature schnauzers. Our salt-and-pepper schnauzer is Buck, and our black schnauzer is called Brandy.

Nancy has them do all of the standard tricks like roll over and jump in the air. She also has a trick where she says, "Bang bang," and Buck immediately falls over dead with paws protruding up in the air. Well, for the most part he is dead. His little tail keeps wagging in anticipation of the treat he is about to receive. But the trick that amazes me the most is when Nancy puts a chunk of tender meat on the bridge of the dogs' little noses and then commands them to stay. I am walking around trying to get them to eat the meat by saying things such as, "Okay. You can eat it" or "Now!" But they do not move. They are like statues. Even though it is in their nature to eat the meat, they continue to balance the meat on their noses until Nancy says, "Okay." Then they scarf it up.

I wondered why they didn't just eat the meat. What kept them from swallowing it up impulsively? I discovered it was their focus. These little dogs never once focused on the meat; they only focused on the master. When the master said it was okay, then they ate—and not until.

Our original parents, Adam and Eve, lost focus. Instead of focusing on the Master, they focused on the meat. We have been given a second chance. Every day you and I are faced with temptation all around us. But thank God, "greater is he that is in [us], than he that is in the world" (1 John 4:4 KJV). "Let us fix our eyes on Jesus, the author and perfecter of our faith" (Heb. 12:2). For in the end we have the promise that "when he appears, we shall be like him" (1 John 3:2).

Personal Evaluation

It is our hope that this chapter has increased your understanding of a fallen person's need for redemption. Let's review what we've learned by restating some key terms from this chapter. Next to each of these terms, write down what it means to you, in your own words. If you can, avoid paging back through the chapter—do it by using your own knowledge!

1. The Fall of man:

   _____

   _____

   _____

2. Total depravity:

   _____

   _____

   _____

3. Our substitute:

   _____

   _____

   _____

4. Trusting Christ as Savior:

_____

_____

_____

5. Forgiveness:

_____

_____

_____

In the Group

1. Could you relate to the opening story of this chapter? Have you ever lost something and longed for its return? If you have and you're comfortable sharing the story with those in your group, do so.

2. What does it mean to you to be made "in the image of God"? Talk about what it means and what it doesn't mean. Do the people you come in contact with every day live like they're in God's image? Why or why not?

3. How do you put together the two concepts of being "in the image of God" and being "totally depraved"? Don't they appear to contradict each other? How is this issue changed by the entrance of Christ into a person's life? How has Christ made a difference in *your* life?

4. Why do you think it is that people run from the concept of death? What are they afraid of? How do you distinguish between spiritual death, physical death, and eternal death?

5. How do you see your salvation at work in your life today? What keeps it a current event rather than simply ancient history? What do you think you could do to make your salvation even

more practically applied in your everyday life? Pool your ideas together as a group.

6. Break off into pairs of prayer partners and share with your partner a request that will help you make your life in Christ a greater reality. Open up, tell him of the issues you struggle with. Ask him to be your prayer partner in order to achieve the success you want in this area. Agree on several practical steps to take this next week. Pray together and then pray for one another all during the week.

Memory Verse: "Therefore if any man be in Christ, he is a new creature, old things are passed away; behold, all things are become new" (2 Cor. 5:17).

Part Three

The Power of Unity

ChapterNine

The Difference Unity Could Make

AT THE PROMISE KEEPERS Conference back in 1992, one of the most outstanding messages to be delivered was by one of the master preachers of our time, Dr. E. V. Hill. He was asked to speak on the Great Commission found at the conclusion of Matthew's Gospel:

> Go therefore and make disciples of all the nations, baptizing them in the name of the Father and the Son and the Holy Spirit, teaching them to observe all that I commanded you, and lo, I am with you always, even to the end of the age. (Matt. 28:19–20 NASB)

Dr. Hill told of a time in our recent history when a political party known as the Black Panthers was having an amazingly effective impact on our country. At the time the famous J. Edgar Hoover was still director of the FBI, and he was especially concerned about this group and its activities.

Hoover assembled a number of leaders from New York City, including Dr. Hill, for the express purpose of discussing the plight of the country as it related to subversive activities. Eventually, the discussion came around to the Black Panther party and its impact on New York City. It was reported to Hoover that the Black Panthers were roaming the streets of New York and as a result stores in some parts of the city were closing at 5 P.M. Report after report confirmed the fact that due to the Black Panthers' activity, fear was beginning to overtake the city.

So Dr. Hill asked a question that he knew the answer to, an answer that he believed everyone else in the room needed to hear: "How many Black Panthers are active in membership here in New York City? How many of them are causing stores to be locked up? How many of them are causing churches not to have worship at night? How many of them are closing down Central Park and Lovers Lane at night? How many of them have gripped the town with fear? What is the active membership of the Black Panther Party of New York?"

The reply sent shock waves and a stunned silence. "Eighty-one."

Dr. Hill began to drive home the point of the story and illustration. "Eighty-one running four million people across the bridges. Eighty-one closing down churches and businesses. Eighty-one causing fear to grip and shutting down the places of social activity. Just eighty-one!" He paused briefly and then continued, "My friends, there needs to be a condemnation of the Black Panthers' activities, but there needs to be a compliment of their *effectiveness.*

Those eighty-one people were dedicated to their cause to the point of risking their own lives. Not caring what could possibly happen to them as a result, they were effective in closing down New York City. In his own powerful style of communicating, Dr. Hill shared, "And I have come here tonight to plead, to beg, that these men of God multiplied eighty-one times will leave here with the Word, so fired up until every city, every community, every church will be turned upside down!"

I've never forgotten that story and probably never will. Can you just imagine if Dr. Hill's request could come true? Wouldn't it be wonderful if we could turn the world upside down for Christ? In a sense, that's what this book has been about. For unity can make that happen.

Transforming Culture

I am firmly of the conviction that we as Christians can change the world. We can transform our culture whether we are eighty-one strong, ten-thousand strong, or all alone. And it is this very transformation that is our mission, our purpose, our reason for being here on this planet.

Men are cause-driven. They are task-driven. They will do anything if they have a clearly defined answer to the question, "Why?" On the other hand, I believe there are many men in the background today because they don't know why we're here and what the church is all about.

That's why a book about what we believe is so very important. It clarifies the mission statement that every man so desperately needs in life. Unity brings with it a sense of belonging, a sense of identity, a purpose. Unity is achieved by keeping Christ primary in our lives. Then, and only then, will all the other aspects of our lives fit into the right places.

The potential of elevating the ethical standards of our society is incredible. We have the chance to elevate the respect for individuals and for businesses and to strengthen homes. Greater numbers of people will come to Christ because a standard of righteousness is being upheld. Despair is being replaced with hope. Crime is being replaced with respect for others.

Unity in Action

Unity is a word that is used a great deal in our society. Politicians use it in their slogans, unions advertise it in their literature, educators boast that unity will make schools more effective, and even neighborhoods promote unity as a way to beat crime in their areas. But for Christians, unity has a more distinct and unique meaning that goes far beyond alliances for the betterment of a community or a nation.

For the Christian, unity speaks of our common relation to God through faith in the person and work of Jesus Christ and our relationship to one another.

I have traveled to a number of foreign countries to minister over the years. For the most part, these were non-English-speaking countries, meaning that I did not speak their language and they did not speak mine. But what I discovered is that whether I was in India or Spain, Germany or Turkey, regardless of the color of skin or the socioeconomic differences, what mattered was that they have a personal relationship with Jesus Christ, as I do. Knowing that, the sense of family has been immediate.

I agree with Geoffrey Bromiley, who wrote of unity in the church more than thirty years ago:

> There is no human route to the true unity of Christian love. It is not an exotic flowering of the old life under the warmth of Christian preaching and the stimulus of common enterprise. It cannot be manufactured by conferences and conventions and conversations. It is not a supreme if rather intangible factor to which appeal can be made on the human level when everything else fails. It is a real unity, contradicting the contradiction of the disunity of jealousy and hatred and anger and bitterness, as the given unity of those who are loved by the one God, and in virtue of His loving action love Him in return, and in so doing are united in love for one another.
>
> Unity in love is unity in the Spirit, and therefore in the Father and the Son. As such it is a true and unbreakable and eternal unity on which we can rest, but on which we must also build, in face of the monstrous challenge of disunity in the world or even in the church. The ultimate fact about us as Christians is that we are united in love whatever appearances may say to the contrary. It is here that we must begin, i.e., in Him who first loved us and whom we therefore love. And beginning here, in this real fact, we can move on with confidence and compulsion to our concrete expressions in the Spirit of this imperishable unity of love.[1]

Using this "higher form" of the word *unity*, let's examine some practical ways to apply unity in our everyday work and world. Recently, I was given a series of questions first asked by J. Robert Nelson in a book he wrote back in the 1950s. I found the issues very thought-provoking in developing a practical strategy on applying unity in our everyday lives.

Promoting Unity

It's one thing to read these doctrines and pleas for unity. But that is just the beginning. It is quite another issue to apply these things. What are some specific ways by which I, as an individual Christian, can promote unity within my local church congregation?

First of all, it is essential that you examine your relationships within your local church. The Lord Jesus told us that we are not to bring sacrifice to the altar if we have something against our brothers. That means that my worship of God, my spiritual growth, and my development are hindered by unresolved issues. As much as we often like to believe or try to convince ourselves that we are "contending for the faith," most of the difficulties within the relationships in the local church and within our denominations or associations have more to do with personal tastes and preference than with biblical truth.

I remember in my first pastorate, I thought it would be a good idea to give everyone the opportunity to have input on the choice of colors for the new hymnals we were about to purchase. *Wrong!* For my entire tenure there I heard about how we listened to the wrong people and how the new hymnals clashed with the sanctuary decor.

I couldn't believe that people could carry on and get so absorbed over the color of a hymnal. In another church I pastored, it took over a year to get new choir robes. The reason for the delay was that the committee couldn't agree on the color. Hurt feelings and fractured relationships result from relatively insignificant issues. Let's face it, these issues pale when they are put next to the reality of the eternal destiny of men and women. Yet how many of us are spending more time and energy on picking colors than on living and communicating Jesus?

So a second aspect of promoting unity is intimately tied in with the first one. I must be willing to put aside nonessential issues of taste and preference to demonstrate the power of biblical unity. The apostle Paul calls this "preferring my brother" or viewing another as "more important."

A friend of mine tells the true story of how a church nearly split over the style of music used in the worship service. More specifically, he tells of how two friends almost parted company over this issue. Brian was of the old school . . . the great and timeless hymns of the faith, the majestic sound of a pipe organ, and a grand choir resplendent in its purple and gold robes. Larry, on the other hand, was an advocate of a more contemporary style of worship. Modern praise choruses played by a band of guitarists and a drummer were more to his liking, and he liked to attend services dressed in casual clothes in a more informal manner.

Fortunately, the church resolved this issue by having the traditional Sunday morning service for those of Brian's tastes and a more contemporary Saturday night service for those of Larry's ilk. That helped the church heal, but Brian and Larry remained distanced for a long time afterward.

It took the death of a mutual friend to reunite the two. At his memorial service, Duane had requested a number of his favorite songs to be sung. It turned out to be a blend of the old hymns and contemporary choruses. As Brian and Larry sang these songs, they realized Duane was giving them one last gift to remember him by.

"I guess I've been kinda stubborn about this music stuff," Brian admitted rather sheepishly to Larry.

"We've *both* been stubborn," Larry corrected.

"And what's really crazy is that it's just not that important an issue!" Brian added.

"I agree, Brian, and I want to apologize to you for bringing such friction into our relationship. To be honest, I've really missed our times together, and I'd like to see if we could start meeting together again on Wednesday mornings for breakfast, like we used to."

Brian and Larry shook hands, then wrapped their arms around each other in a big bear hug. Examining their own personal relationships had brought them together again in unity.

Avoiding the Wrong Path

How can we be sure the movements we make toward closer unity of Christian brothers will not take us down the wrong road? We have seen that Jesus was not referring to an organizational unity but rather a unity of heart and purpose. That definition must remain uppermost in our thinking as we make the issue of unity a personal one.

For example, I have been very excited about the movement some denominations have made over certain issues. Some of these very denominations had split in the past over the issue of race, for instance.

Now they are talking of reuniting, and in the process, great healing of past hurts is taking place. I commend this type of activity.

However, it would be a mistake to extrapolate this to mean that all denominations and independent groups should merge together into some sort of superchurch.

To guard against this, I would propose that we continue to look at unity in relational terms rather than organizational ones. Put another way, I must be committed to developing and maintaining healthy relationships. This endeavor will keep me on the right path.

The Issue of Loyalty

Sometimes when the subject of unity is discussed, a legitimate question is raised about loyalty. On what basis do we decide, if necessary, between loyalty to a brother in Christ who lives in our town but is of a different denomination, and loyalty to the members, traditions, and teachings of our own denomination in other parts of the world?

We must always keep in mind that we have one primary relationship that must not be sacrificed for anything, and that is our relationship with Jesus Christ. He is the One to whom we owe allegiance.

As J. I. Packer has said, "It's about time for Christians who recite the creed and mean it to come together for fellowship and witness regardless of denominational identity."[2]

In terms of getting along with others, this is probably a good time to add that we need to avoid the position of saying, "unity will take place when *they* get *their* act together." An organization tends to be run from the top down, which is a view that allows most of us to complain, since we're mostly at the bottom. We'll gripe, malign those at the top, and place the blame for all that ails the church on them.

However, if I view the church as the body of Christ, a living organism, then I have just as much responsibility as everyone else to participate. It is not a matter of blame and shame but rather an issue of taking personal responsibility of where I may be.

This means I can begin to be a bridge builder with others within the body of Christ. We can seek to work together in our community to be salt and light. Being willing to unite on our common faith and to impact the world is what should be our goal. Again, this is *relational* unity, not *organizational.* This means I have the ability to begin with one believer and then another and then another. Perhaps the best place to begin is within my own local church. Ask yourself the question, "Have I allowed others the freedom to disagree in nonessential areas of truth?"

In the midst of this celebration of bridge-building, remember the words of Peter, who said we must obey God rather than man.

Dealing with Differences

What if there are legitimate differences that separate brothers? In all our talk of unity, this issue of disagreement must be addressed further. In my thinking, the relationship of the brothers is of prime importance, so it is important to place it in the context of the following suggestions.

The key issue is *identification.* By that I mean it is imperative to identify exactly what it is that is causing the difference in thinking. In identifying the issue, it is helpful to clarify if it is a *primary* issue or a *secondary* issue.

A primary issue is one that has as its basis one of the five fundamentals of the faith that we've presented in this book. It's the sort of issue that caused Paul to warn the elders in Ephesus before his departure: "Keep watch over yourselves and all the flock of which the Holy Spirit has made you overseers" (Acts 20:28a).

If someone disagrees with us in one of the five fundamentals, Matthew 18 also comes into play. The so-called believer who does not hold to the truth is committing sin—specifically the sin of heresy—and therefore he or she must be put out of the local church fellowship and/or the denomination. It's not our desire to discipline someone in sin and to cut off fellowship, but given a lack of repentance we are left with no other choice when it concerns a primary issue of Scripture.

This includes the person who claims to affirm the basics but also affirms the opposite at the same time—for example, people who say they believe in Christ but also trust in some sort of works to get them to heaven. (Remember, salvation is by Christ alone!)

For additional Scripture on dealing with the primary issues, see Romans 16:17–18; 2 Thessalonians 3:14–15; 1 Timothy 6:20; and 2 Timothy 4:14.

But there are also issues that are not of the magnitude of violating one of the fundamentals of the faith. They would be placed in the category of secondary issues, and thus, Matthew 18 would not be the applicable Scripture. For these sorts of disagreements Romans 14 and 15 would come into focus. Keeping the Sabbath, eating meat once sacrificed to idols, commemorating pagan holidays, and similar issues were the secondary topics of the New Testament era. Paul had a plan that worked.

The plan is this: "Let us therefore make every effort to do what leads to peace and to mutual edification" (Rom. 14:19). In other words, it is my brother who is important, not the issue. The focus should be on two brothers trying to get along, not fighting. This passage is also helpful in how it removes the idea of *judgment* from the discussion. It's removed from both sides . . . it's not important. What is important is acknowledging the importance of the relationship.

We need to fight the urge to say in haste, "This is what I believe . . . for this is God's view, and you therefore are sinning!" We must be careful to identify what is a primary and what is a secondary issue. I realize this is tough for many of us, but it is absolutely essential to the unity of the body.

Unity and Individual Expression

Every Christian is called to work out his or her own salvation with fear and trembling. Although this verse has caused its share of confusion, it at least means that there will be diversity in the way in which this happens. For instance, one Christian may be called to minister in rural communities while another will feel called to the inner city. Another believes he or she should give away all material possessions to the poor while another gives generously while living in an upscale community, reaching out to a group of people many of us will never come in contact with.

The danger is when I start to believe that the way I am doing it is the "Christian way," implying all others are incorrect. I have a friend, for example, who is an African-American. He has been challenged on numerous occasions that if he were really sold on ministering to his people, he would relocate to the inner city to minister in that context. The problem is, only God has the right to tell him to do that and, so far, He hasn't.

We fall on dangerous ground when we assume that our culture, our politics, or our social issues must be held by "all good, Bible-believing Christians." This also leads to the issue of racial diversity as well.

Racial Unity

Is the power of Christian love strong enough to defeat the divisive powers of racial and cultural conflict? Racial strife is contrary to the nature of Christ, and therefore it is contrary to the essential nature of the church.

In our society there has been much discussion (and rightly so) concerning racial issues and racial reconciliation. While I agree with many of the laws that have been passed and the programs that have been instituted, I'm afraid that ultimately they will have very little power to change anything. Why? Because racism is an issue of *the head, the heart, and the hands.*

What is needed is an understanding of what God says, a transformation of the *head,* if you will. We need to appreciate the fact that we are all created in God's image and recreated in the image of Christ.

Next is the *heart,* meaning a love that comes from understanding God's great love for us, that while we were yet sinners, Christ died for us. Then that love needs to be applied!

We apply love with our *hands.* Practicing thoughtful acts of love and friendship is a powerful tool.

One man building a relationship with another man across racial barriers, demonstrating the love and power of God, will impact a home, and that home will impact a community, and that community will impact a nation. The power of the church and the love of God work things out from the bottom up, not the top down. This is how to be one of Dr. Hill's "eighty-one." It will make a difference . . . and it's a difference that will last through eternity.

The Power of Prayer

When you think about it, if God's desire is unity, how can we as Christians not be coming before God in prayer, regularly asking Him to heal our divisions and enable us to work together? Shouldn't we be echoing the Lord's prayer, "that they may be one"?

A number of exciting things are happening in the United States and in other parts of the world in the whole area of prayer. It seems that wherever I travel, I hear of prayer movements that are crossing all the man-made barriers within the church. Concerts of prayer, prayer summits, Christians praying for their neighborhoods, and days of prayer and fasting are some of the actions that are occurring, all being sponsored by local churches and national or international ministries.

Prayer and worship are great equalizers. They bring all of us to the foot of the cross, and there we see who is important: the Lord Jesus. It is when we come before God in worship and prayer that we see Him high and lifted up, as the Scripture states in Isaiah 6. We see our sin of self and are able to see more clearly the needs of our brothers. It is then that we say, "Lord, here am I, send me" (v. 8 KJV).

Nothing that is blessed of God starts, continues, or comes to a positive end without prayer. It is *the* place to start when it comes to expressing the unity that is ours in Christ.

Conclusion

A number of years ago I was invited to attend a meeting of pastors from across the country. The purpose of the conference was to provide opportunity for discussion on a variety of topics related to ministry and to build up relationships within the group. At first, I decided not to go because of previous and pressing issues, but at the urging of a friend, I changed my schedule in order to attend.

Upon arrival I met pastors from a variety of denominations, some of which I had never heard of before. I was assigned to room with a pastor from Texas, who seemed very uneasy the entire first day of the conference. When we retired to our room that evening, we exchanged pleasantries, and suddenly he blurted out that he needed to talk with me and he hoped I would be willing to listen!

I wasn't sure what was going on here, and quite honestly, I didn't really want to stay up all night in order to be grilled theologically by this man. However, before I could even respond, he started firing questions at me.

He had a lot of questions concerning denominations, asking me my opinion on many that were represented at this conference. I answered his questions the best I could, and I listened as he shared concerning his denomination, his upbringing, and his pastorate. Our talk went deep into the night, and finally we collapsed into our beds in the early-morning hours.

The first session the following morning, my roommate asked the leader of the session if he could say a few words. He rose to his feet and was immediately overcome with tears, rendering him unable to speak for several minutes. Finally, he addressed the group, saying, "I was raised to believe that only those who were a part of my denomination were truly saved. While I had left that belief intellectually a number of years ago, it wasn't until last night that I left it emotionally."

Then he paused and added, "Would you all please forgive me?"

The freedom and power that came into that man's ministry were enormous! He came out of isolation and into relationship for the glory of God.

That's what this book has been all about. As we started with the account of Coach McCartney leading a stadium full of men in affirming all the pastors, allow me to add a personal footnote to that story.

The night of that amazing event was also the night I was in the hospital recovering from what I had thought was my heart attack. One of the last things I did before going to the hospital was to share a few moments with Coach Mac. I had promised him that I would pray for his message that night in Boulder, and I stayed true to my word. When

Susan arrived at the hospital, I kept telling her that we needed to pray for Coach Mac, because I had promised. Later, Susan would tell me that I was mumbling this same phrase over and over, a result of the doctor's heavy medication.

After the medication had worn off a bit, I once again regained my senses. I asked Susan if she knew of any way to find out what was going on at the stadium. She called one of my friends and coworkers who was at the stadium. He told her to put the hospital phone up to my ear, and as I did so he held his cellular phone up in the middle of a balcony out at the end of the stadium. We had no idea what was happening, but soon it became clear that we were hearing a sound like we had never heard before—the men cheering the pastors and chanting, "We love you! We love you!"

The awesome power of shared beliefs was being evidenced! Men of every race, denomination, and nondenominational group were coming together to affirm pastors without regard to the color of their skin or their theological labels. All that was important was that there was a core set of beliefs held in common, and based on those, the body of Christ would reach out. As those men in the stands began to shout, "We love you! We love you!" and as the pastors responded the same way, I sat in my hospital bed and wept.

I wept because Paul's heart, as revealed in Romans 15:5–6, was being evidenced. I wept because many were seeing for the first time the truth of our Lord's prayer in John 17. I then began to wonder, *What if men went home to their churches committed even to the point of death to the core doctrines of the faith?*

What if men went home to their churches committed to show love to one another and to their pastor, demonstrating grace on nonprimary issues?

What if pastors chose to maintain healthy discussions with fellow pastors about secondary issues but also committed to work together, holding fast to shared beliefs?

What would happen in our urban and suburban and rural churches and communities if this really happened?

What would happen in our nation if true Christians knelt together in prayer and rose up to preach the gospel and to live out the gospel together?

Yes, I can't help but wonder . . . How about you?

The awesome power of shared beliefs doesn't come from the signing of a statement or even assenting that the statements are true. The awesome power of shared beliefs will only become reality when we come together, based on these beliefs, with a unity of purpose and witness to a lost world.

Personal Evaluation

Since this is our last chapter, let's use it as a time to review what we have learned together. Look back over the chapters and reflect on two key issues for each topic. Jot down the most significant truth you learned from each chapter. After that, write down a specific way you can apply something from each chapter as well.

1. "Friendly Fire"
   The most significant truth I learned is

   _____
   _____

   I can apply what I learned by

   _____
   _____

2. "That They May Be One"
   The most significant truth I learned is

   _____
   _____

   I can apply what I learned by

   _____
   _____

3. "The Faith Once for All Entrusted"
   The most significant truth I learned is

   _____

   _____

   I can apply what I learned by

   _____

   _____

4. "The Bible"
   The most significant truth I learned is

   _____

   _____

   I can apply what I learned by

   _____

   _____

5. "God"
   The most significant truth I learned is

   _____

   _____

   I can apply what I learned by

   _____

   _____

6. "Jesus Christ"
   The most significant truth I learned is

   _____

   _____

   I can apply what I learned by

   _____

   _____

7. "The Holy Spirit"
   The most significant truth I learned is

   _____

   _____

   I can apply what I learned by

   _____

   _____

8. "The Redemption of Man"
   The most significant truth I learned is

   _____

   _____

   I can apply what I learned by

   _____

   _____

9. "The Difference Unity Could Make"
   The most significant truth I learned is

   _____

   _____

   I can apply what I learned by

   _____

   _____

In the Group

1. As a group, share as many ideas as you can on how to promote unity in your specific area. What are some positive things that can be done right away? What are the potential obstacles that must be overcome? What is the best strategy to overcome them?

2. Have you ever faced a situation where you had to determine your loyalty to a church or denomination or association? How

did you decide to whom to be loyal? Were you misunderstood by some? How did you deal with the criticism that may have resulted? Share as freely with the group as you are comfortable. We can all learn from each other's experiences.

3. What about individual expression? Why is it that our culture tends to "box in" people, saying if they are of a certain background they should minister in a certain way? What is the danger of people believing that their way is the only way? Is there any Scripture that comes to mind for this issue?

4. What are you doing personally to ensure unity among the races? Each of you share as many answers to this question as you are able. What do you think it will take for men to see how vitally important this issue is? How would you teach your sons and daughters about racial unity and equality? What would you stress as important to them?

5. Why is prayer important to unity? How have the prayer times of this group been a positive effect in your life, personally? Have you experienced the supernatural power of prayer in a recent life situation? Share your insights with the group.

6. Conclude your session with a season of prayer as a group. Ask the Lord to empower you to fulfill the unity we all seek. Tell God of your desire to be one of the handful—one of the eighty-one—who wants to contribute to turning the world upside down for Christ. Thank God for the members of this group and, in particular, for your prayer partner over the last few months. If you desire to do so, don't conclude this session without making arrangements for staying in contact with one another!

Memory Verse: "How good and pleasant it is when brothers live together in unity!" (Ps. 133:1 NIV).

Notes

Chapter 1. Friendly Fire

1. Condensed from Jeris E. Bragan, "Friendly Fire," *Christian Herald Magazine,* July–August 1991, 20–23.
2. George Verwer, *Hunger for Reality* (Carlisle, U.K.: Operation Mobilization, 1993), 91 (originally published by Tyndale House in 1972 as *Come! Live! Die!*). Used with permission of George Verwer.
3. Condensed from Charles Colson with Ellen Santilli Vaughn, *The Body* (Dallas: Word, 1992), 186.
4. Bruce and Marshall Shelley, *The Consumer Church: Can Evangelicals Win the World without Losing Their Souls?* (Downers Grove, Ill.: InterVarsity, 1992), 109.
5. Colson, *The Body,* 102.
6. *Joint Warfare of the U.S. Armed Forces* (Washington, D.C.: National Defense University Press, 1991), ii.

Chapter 2. That They May Be One

1. Charles Schulz, "Peanuts" comic strip, cited in Bruce L. Shelley, *What Is the Church?* (Wheaton, Ill.: Victor, 1978), 38.
2. William Hendriksen, *The Gospel of John,* a volume in the New Testament Commentary series (Grand Rapids: Baker, 1953; ninth printing, 1981), 364–5.

3. Leon Morris, *The Gospel According to John* (Grand Rapids: Eerdmans, 1971), 734–5.
4. Colson, *The Body,* 104.
5. Karen Mains, *The Key to an Open Heart* (Elgin, Ill.: David C. Cook, 1979), 143–4.

Chapter 3. The Faith Once for All Entrusted

1. *Joint Warfare of the U.S. Armed Forces,* 371.
2. Jim Petersen, *Church without Walls* (Colorado Springs: NavPress, 1992), 87.
3. Simon J. Kistemaker, *New Testament Commentary: Exposition Of the Epistles of Peter and of the Epistle of Jude* (Grand Rapids: Baker, 1987), 371.
4. Ibid., 32.

Chapter 4. The Bible *by Dr. Bruce L. Shelly*

1. The Story of Bishop Felix is from Herbert Workman's *Persecution in the Early Church* (London: Epworth, 1923), 275.
2. Clyde S. Kilby, ed., *An Anthology of C. S. Lewis* (New York: Harcourt, Brace, and World, 1969), 23.
3. C. S. Lewis, *Reflections on the Psalms* (New York: Harcourt, Brace, and World, 1958), 116–17.

Chapter 5. God *by Dr. Max Anders*

1. Deidre Sullivan, *What Do We Mean When We Say "God"?* (New York: Doubleday, 1990), 95.
2. Alister McGrath, *Understanding the Trinity* (Grand Rapids: Academic Books, 1988), 110.
3. Condensed from Harold Kushner, *Who Needs God?* (New York: Summit Books, 1989), 9–11.

Chapter 8. The Redemption of Man *by Dr. Rod Cooper*

1. R. C. Sproul, *Essential Truths of the Christian Faith* (Wheaton, Ill.: Tyndale House, 1992), 132.
2. Charles C. Ryrie, *Basic Theology* (Wheaton, Ill.: Victor, 1986), 191.

3. Max Lucado, *In the Eye of the Storm* (Dallas: Word, 1991).

4. Bruce L. Shelley, *Theology for Ordinary People* (Downers Grove, Ill.: InterVarsity, 1993).

5. Sproul, *Essential Truths*, 144.

6. Charles Swindoll, *Growing Deep in the Christian Life* (Portland, Ore.: Multnomah, 1987), 97–98.

Chapter 9. The Difference Unity Could Make

1. Geoffrey William Bromiley, *The Unity and Disunity of the Church* (Grand Rapids: Eerdmans, 1958), 52–53.

2. J. I. Packer, quoted in Colson, *The Body*.